Groomed

First published in Great Britain by Simon & Schuster UK Ltd, 2012
A CBS COMPANY

1 3 5 7 9 10 8 6 4 2

Simon & Schuster UK Ltd
1st Floor
222 Gray's Inn Road
London WC1X 8HB

www.simonandschuster.co.uk

Simon & Schuster Australia, Sydney
Simon & Schuster India, New Delhi

A CIP catalogue record for this book
is available from the British Library.

ISBN 978-0-85720-827-9

Typeset in Bell by M Rules
Printed and bound by CPI Group (UK) Ltd, Croydon, CR0 4YY

Groomed

An uncle who went too far.
A mother who didn't care.
A little girl who waited years for justice.

LAURIE MATTHEW

**SIMON &
SCHUSTER**

London · New York · Sydney · Toronto · New Delhi

A CBS COMPANY

Dedicated to two very special people in my life:
my little sister Sharron – who always tried to tell –
and my youngest daughter Jerricah –
who was the one who said I finally should.

The poems at the start of each chapter were written by Laurie during the years of her abuse. She has the originals and has transcribed them exactly as she wrote them down during those horrific years.

CONTENTS

INTRODUCTION

ORDINARY

My name is Laurie Matthew and I am about to tell you things that I have never told anyone else.

When you read my story – a story I have chosen to keep quiet about for many years, for reasons which will become apparent very soon – you won't want to believe it. I know that. I know it because, in my work, in every day of my life, I deal with terrible stories of awful things done to children that no one wants to believe. Why would this be any different?

In fact, you'll find this one even harder to believe. There will be times when you will think it so fantastical, so unlikely, that you'll wonder how anyone could have thought of doing what was done to me. But they did.

I work in an ordinary place but I deal with extraordinary people every day. This story begins with the ordinary – but that won't last for long.

Some years ago, I set up a charity for survivors of child abuse. The charity has grown and evolved, but one thing has stayed the same: from one day to the next I never know what to expect. However, the people who walk through our doors – girls, boys, women, men, mums, dads, doctors, lawyers, addicts, teachers, anyone you can think of – all have one thing in common: they're still standing. And, for some, that is an incredible achievement. Without exception, the journey they have taken has been a long one, a horrific one, and it's still continuing. It will continue every day of their lives, even when they have happy days, good days, days they thought they would never have again. I am one of these survivors, even if many of them don't realise it. It isn't my place to tell them my story. I'm there to listen, not talk.

I don't like attention. I like to be quiet, to fade into the background. I'll do everything in my power to help the people who come to me, though, and, for them, I'll go beyond my comfort zone. I will talk. I will be the one who stands up and gives speeches. I will draw attention to myself. I can do it if it's for someone else or a cause, but I don't like it, and I certainly have never done it for myself before. So, you'll have to bear with me. This isn't something which comes naturally to me, but I'm doing it for a reason.

Each day, I sit in my office – in the background there's always a kettle on, there's always a phone ringing, there's always someone coming in to ask something, chat to someone, or even just to look at the chinchillas we keep. The tears are often hidden, but the laughter isn't. We're a friendly bunch, I hope. We help, we listen. Sometimes we say nothing because sometimes that is exactly what's needed.

I've been doing this job for many years now. I've set up services and groups. I talk to politicians and teachers. I give evidence and run training programmes. I can hardly remember all of the countries I've visited, the people I've met.

Of course, things stick in my mind, and that day six years ago is one that always will. I sat in the same office I've just mentioned and, just like every afternoon, the kettle was on and the phones were ringing. I picked up the local newspaper and looked at the headline. Another abuser, another story of childhoods shattered and innocence ripped to pieces.

The headline this time screamed of justice – it was a historical case of two little girls who had been abused by a family member, but who had finally spoken up and finally secured some degree of justice.

The man who had been found guilty of these hideous crimes over many, many years was nothing special. He was old, a pensioner. There was nothing remarkable about him. In my experience, there rarely is.

As I continued to look at the story, it all seemed so familiar. I had heard it all so many times before. I was used to it. I was used to abusers looking like everyone else. I was used to the fact that they had normal jobs, normal lives, and were often thought of as upstanding citizens. I was used to all of this.

What I wasn't used to was the fact that, this time, it was my name in the newspaper.

I was the one identified as the victim.

It was my uncle who had been convicted.

This time, I was the story.

I had dedicated my life to trying to make a difference, to helping others who had been through this awful experience, but I had never spoken about what I had lived through.

This time was different.

This time, it was all about me.

CHAPTER 1

FAMILY

I don't care when you shout and hurt.
I'll never cry for you.
My tears are mine, mine to cry inside,
Where I hide from you and you and you.

I was born into very ordinary surroundings. Of course, what was 'ordinary' in 1950s working-class Dundee would be seen as downright poverty these days. Our house was small and damp with windows that rattled. Water would run down the inside of them and pool on the wooden window ledge. We had outside toilets, no street lights and the only heating came from a coal fire. That fire had a ledge for the kettle which could be pushed over the fire, with a brass coal scuttle and a brass container for the poker, tongs and small brush and shovel for cleaning the fire at the side. We washed with carbolic soap and there were no tooth-brushes. Double glazing was something none of us had heard of, and you could only keep warm in winter by wrapping layers of rough blankets around you. There were no

1

phones, no television. The floors didn't have carpets and the furnishings were sparse, to say the least.

The front room had a deep sink, a wooden table and wooden chairs and a sideboard full of bits and pieces. There was linoleum on the floor and a bed in the bed recess. Inside the front door was a small, dark lobby which housed the coin-operated electric meter. There was one more room, a back one, that had no light coming into it at all, unless the electric one was switched on. Children were certainly never allowed to put the light on as it cost too much money. This back room housed the Singer sewing machine on a black stand, a wooden dresser for clothing, and a cupboard that had all the bedding in it. A mattress on the floor became the 'shackydoon', my bed. It was folded away to make space in the morning and the floor was bare. The walls in the front room were painted a pink colour with flying ducks, a mirror and various pictures. The back room was very shabby, with walls covered in peeling, wafer-thin lining paper, and an overwhelming smell of damp.

In the winter, we didn't even have gloves – but children would wrap their hands in rags or socks to keep the cold out. I didn't know anyone who had more than one set of 'real' clothes and shoes; hand-me-downs were commonplace, and even Sunday best was often second-hand. Most women knitted, but that didn't mean that they were any good at it! Even young children were taught how to mend or darn and, again, this often resulted in some real raggle-taggle outfits. In fact, no matter their age, all children would be encouraged, expected really, to help with household chores.

This could include washing potatoes (they were never peeled as this would be a waste), cleaning and laying the fire, cutting up newspaper to be used as loo roll, and doing a hundred other little things every day. There were no washing machines or microwaves or toasters. In fact, given that toast was made at the fire, one of the jobs often given to kids was to scrape the black bits off. The whole lot smelled because of the stench from the coal fires which permeated everything – but everyone smelled the same.

The skyline was totally different back then, too. There were no TV aerials, no phone wires (because there were no phones in the homes of poor folk), no satellite dishes – no signs of the so-called 'civilisation' that today's society takes for granted.

This was the world into which I was born. By the time I came along, my parents already had one child, a boy who was fourteen months older than me. He was the reason for them marrying in the first place. No one needed to tell me this; as soon as I could count and knew how long babies took to grow, I also knew that George was born less than nine months after they married.

Our flat was in the centre of Dundee, a major city about an hour north of Edinburgh, with a history of jute making and shipping. It was a lifetime ago. Today, Dundee is on the rise. Millions of pounds are being poured into the city. There's a new Victoria and Albert Museum being planned, and the waterfront is developing so fast that there is even talk of a Guggenheim Museum there in twenty years' time.

Back then, when I was a little girl, it couldn't have been more different; there was very little traffic, so no real need to learn about road safety. In the centre of the city, there were more cars than further out in the suburbs and rural areas, but not really that many. All of the cars were the same colour – black. I remember that they had great big grilles on the front and indicators that would come out of the side of them like little flags. There were still trams in Dundee when I was young, as well, and they made up the majority of the traffic, along with bikes and trucks and buses. For the people who did have cars, there were no problems with parking as they could just leave their vehicles wherever they wanted them without fear of double yellow lines or meters. Those things simply didn't exist. The buses were green with hard plastic seats and no doors. They were freezing to sit in and pretty unsafe, too. Health and safety regulations hadn't even been thought of; you took your life in your hands every time you got on a double-decker!

There were lots of small shops, all different and a world away from today, where every high street looks the same and is full of big-name retailers (although we did have a Woolworths). Most of the shops had a pull-down, overhead canopy so that shoppers could stay dry while they looked in the window if it was raining. There were draper's, butcher's, ironmonger's, fruit and vegetable shops. None of them gave out plastic bags – if, for example, you wanted potatoes, they'd be weighed out (in pounds not kilos) and tipped straight into your shopping bag or basket. There were no processed foods, so basic ingredients had to be bought and made into meals. Shops sold things out of big vats, such as broken biscuits, flour and oats. There was no piped music, just the sound of gossip.

The streets had market stalls along the middle and 'gypsies' sold things from baskets. There was one of these markets in the middle of town where my family got a lot of our clothing. It was old stuff, but it would be unpicked and unravelled to be re-knitted and re-sewn into 'new' clothes.

Everyone smoked – even in shops. My parents both smoked; no one had a clue about the health risks. People seemed always to have a fag in their hands or mouths, irrespective of what they were doing, or whether they were around babies or kids – or even pregnant themselves.

In fact, everything stank of one thing or another. The main smells during the day were of the 'steamie', or washroom, which was out the back. The steamie for all the tenements was behind our place, so it was always noisy and frantic. The mixed-up stench that came from it was of carbolic soap, steam and sweat. It was always busy with women and kids doing washing. Sometimes, after the clothes had been done, the kids would be out in the dirty water for a cursory clean, too. I think they came out dirtier than they went in.

There were two outside toilets shared by a lot of people. The whole close consisted of about ten families, and they almost all had kids, so there must have been at least 40 people sharing those two toilets, which was pretty disgusting. The women took turns cleaning it but there were not the cleaning products around that we have now. Carbolic soap and bleach had to do for everything. There was a cistern high up on the wall with a metal chain which you pulled to flush it, and a high toilet with a wooden seat which was pretty difficult for a child to use. The walls were brick and there was no sink. Toilet paper was nothing more than cut-up newspaper that you took in with you each time; you couldn't even leave that there in case someone pinched it. During the night people used a chamber pot, as there were no lights outside and no torches; who would want to risk going out there in the wee small hours?

I don't really remember any neighbours, other than an aunt and uncle who lived in the next close, but there were always people around. The tenement didn't have a secure entry, so the close was open to anyone and to the elements, as well. My mother had a thing about keeping up appearances and regularly stained our front door step a reddish brown colour to make it look posh, as well as scrubbing every other part of the close that she could get her hands on.

The street was long and wide with shops opposite. About 50 yards from us, on the same side, was a builder's yard where my father worked as a bricklayer. It was a street busy with people rather than cars. We were near enough to the River Tay to smell the sea water sometimes and the sound of gulls was a common one.

It was unusual to see a man out and about without a hat

on his head, or a woman without a hat or a headscarf tied into a triangle shape. The boys wore short trousers and the girls wore dresses and ribbons in their hair. There was very little choice, but no one thought anything of it; it was just the way things were.

I shared my bedroom with my brother George when he wasn't in hospital. He was born with a lung problem and then contracted diphtheria and was also diagnosed as having an issue with his spine. He was a stranger to me. The hospital was about 40 miles away and it was impossible for working-class people like us to reach. Although my dad could drive, he only did so at work; we had no car, so they didn't go to see George very often.

I knew very little of what was going on with George. In those days, kids weren't really brought into family discussions. Things went on around you, but you had to try and join the dots of the story yourself. The old adage of children being seen and not heard was very much the constant rule. So I have few memories of George. I actually thought that he lived in hospital and that it was unusual when he was at home, rather than the other way around. I didn't know anything different, this was just how my world was. I simply lived my life, rarely with my brother there, and sometimes with the next-door uncle, aunt and their child.

My family didn't have a lot but neither did anyone else around us. There were no holidays, no visits to the park or beach or cinema. The only 'toys' I had were stones picked up on the street, or bits of wood or coal that had fallen from trucks or carts. I remember playing in the gutters during the rain with stones and wood and bits of paper, seeing what would float.

The area we lived in was dark; there was no street or close lighting and the smoke from the chimneys stained everything black, including the trees. It was poor, austere and miserable. People were serious, tired from working and they tended not to play with children or encourage children to play with each other either. If you were spotted sitting about, someone would find you a job to do. Even old folk sitting in the street on a nice day would drag you over to shell peas or they'd put a hank of wool on your arms so they could wind it into a ball.

Dad was a brickie but Mum never really had a career as such; a combination of the times, my brother's illness and her 'not having the temperament', as she would put it. She would occasionally work in shops and clean offices. I know she was a seamstress as well, at some point, and took in mending work, but there was no one profession which she stuck at. Looking back at the type of person she was, I suspect that this 'temperament' affected more people than just myself, although I also suspect I was the one who was most affected by it.

Mum's mood was the yardstick by which I measured most of my life in those days. To say she had a temper was an understatement. One day, when I was quite little, she tried to show me how to knit (again, this was the sort of thing every child I knew would have done, it was just part of contributing to the household). I had real difficulty managing it as I must have been only about four at the time.

'God, you're stupid,' she snapped, as her hand slapped the side of my head.

This went on for some time. I kept trying – but I just couldn't do it. I don't know whether it was because I was too little, useless at knitting, or so wary of how she was going to respond that I couldn't settle, but I do know that her anger boiled up higher and higher every time I failed to cast on, and with every dropped stitch.

The same thing happened when she tried to show me how to do simple stitching. I accidentally stuck the needle into my finger and bled onto the sampler cloth.

'Is there anything you can do right?' she shouted. 'I don't know why I bother. You're useless – always have been and always will be.'

It was a long way from being a romantic, rosy-eyed childhood. I knew that we were quite deprived, but I also knew that most of our neighbours were, too. They dressed the same way, they ate the same things, and they just got by from week to week, sometimes from day to day. No one was flash or had a lot of money to throw about. Everyone seemed to work in shops, factories or on building sites, even if it was just a few hours here and there, or for very little money. It was considered pretty shameful to be unemployed, especially for men, and people would speak about them and call them 'kettle boilers' and suchlike.

However, despite the similarities in many ways with other

households, I always felt different and it was a difference which didn't come from a lack of material things. Our house was in an area in which everyone lived close to each other, so you could always see how other families lived and treated their kin. I watched how others were raised and it was nothing like my own experience. I saw them being hugged and wondered why I never got that. I saw their mums give them a wee slap for being cheeky, but not nearly break their jaw in anger, like my mum. When they had a row, I looked on as mums would cuddle their children straightaway afterwards, as if they regretted having to discipline them. They'd wipe the dirt from their faces, and take them inside for their tea. When a child fell over or got into a fight, one of their parents usually came out and picked them up or argued with any neighbour who was trying to discipline them.

On the whole, people minded their own business in those days. Children belonged to the parents and no one meddled in other families. It was a different time when parents could, and did, batter their child in the street without anyone saying or doing anything. These days, they do it behind closed doors. However, there was also a tribal possessiveness with some parents, whereby they might knock seven shades out of their own kid, but they wouldn't have anyone else say a thing about them.

It wasn't like that for me. Even at the age of three, I would be sitting on the pavement, dreading the thought of going back home. Adults would see me, I guess, but they wouldn't interfere because of this unwritten 1950s working-class law that you kept your nose out. I started learning to watch other people from that moment in my life, and it was something I never gave up. I do it to this day. Whenever I've felt that I don't quite know how to act or react, I study others, I study 'normal' people for clues, and I try to do what they do, because I was never able to learn how to behave in society the way other children were.

I always felt on the outside. I always felt hungry and a bit miserable. It was common practice (not just for me) to send a child to bed without tea as a punishment. Food was in short supply in general and you were grateful for what you were given. I never saw being hungry as something wrong. It was just how it was. Kids were low down the pecking order and the dad and breadwinner would get the best food without question. Kids in those days rarely got breakfast, dinner, tea, love and support. Perhaps two of these out of the whole list at a push!

I wasn't a child who smiled; in fact there isn't a single photograph of me with so much as a hint of a grin on my face. And was it any wonder? My life was horrible, I knew that then and I know it now, looking back with an adult's awareness. Smiling in young children tends to be in response to someone smiling at them, but that didn't happen much in my life.

Mum seemed to be incapable of showing me love, and she wasn't the only one. My granny on Dad's side used to glare at me with absolute hatred in her eyes. She always made it clear to me that it should have been me in the hospital and not my beautiful brother, as she called George. When I was very young, I never understood but, as time went on, I often had comments thrown at me about being healthy and well, while George suffered and was fragile.

One day, my mum said, looking at me with cold eyes, 'It should have been you, by God, it should have been you,' as she discussed George with Granny Matthew.

The comment my mum made was repeated a lot. Perhaps if I hadn't been born they'd have had more money and been able to visit George more often. Perhaps it was all about him being a boy and the firstborn, and yet it was the girl who was fit and healthy. I was the one they could focus all their anger on when they thought about George's illness, so in that way I was the scapegoat. In fact, their dislike of me was the only thing that brought my mum and Gran together. Gran was Protestant and Mum was Church of England – which, in the eyes of working-class Scots at that time, was as good as Catholic. They never saw eye-to-eye on anything except their love for George, and their dislike of me.

I have no idea why this was their way of thinking. That I was so hated by the two women who should have adored me was proof, in my eyes, that I was unworthy of being loved in the first place. Mums and grans automatically adore little girls, don't they? I thought they did. I thought they should. It was what I saw all around me, but none of it applied to me. Given that neither of them felt that way about me must mean that it was my fault, I reasoned.

Granny Matthew would pinch me and push me. She didn't even do it in private; she would quite openly shove me or hurt me in front of others. I would see her being loving with my cousin who lived in the next close. He was older than me and when she visited, she would hug and kiss him and say that she loved him. She was affectionate to my father and uncles, too, and would hug them when they met. Why could no one ever feel that way towards me, I wondered?

Every time we went into her house, my mum would nudge me and say, 'Give your granny a kiss.'

'Look at her, look at how slow she is, bloody idiot,' my gran would say as I walked over. 'Get her away from me!' she'd shudder as I bent to kiss her cheek. 'Go on, get that fat idiot out of my sight!' she'd shriek, pushing me away.

I never cried at these words – I was a very stoical child, but my lack of tears gave them more ammunition.

'Does she ever react?' my gran would say. 'I think she's slow, that one – you don't even get a bloody tear from her.'

If I had said anything, Mum would have battered me anyway. You had to respect adults back then; no talking back, speak when spoken to, and all of those rules, irrespective of what the adult was doing or saying. Anyway, crying only works if someone cares enough to notice. I learned from a very young age that there was no point.

My mum was always threatening to 'give me something to cry about'. She'd call me names and never show a hint of affection. She didn't just ignore me, she went out of her way to show how much she disliked me. I wasn't just invisible to her; she would look at me like I was something disgusting. Any time George was home from hospital, she would shower him with love and attention, and make it very clear to the whole family, by saying it constantly, that he was her favourite – I simply couldn't compete. I don't know how it had all become that way; I just accepted it. I wasn't my brother and I was a poor substitute. I've tried to work out how a toddler can bring out such hatred in adults and I really can't fathom it. If I'd been older and if I'd been 'bad', then maybe they would have had an excuse, but how can you be this way with someone who is little more than a baby? What could I possibly have done to make them dislike me so?

One day, when I was three, Granny Matthew gave me a pram. It was a real pram, for a real baby, not for a dolly, and there was a tremendous fuss made of the fact that she was being so generous. It was actually in an absolute state and only fit for the dump, but it was presented to me as if it was made of gold, and I was expected to be terribly grateful.

'Look at that, Lorraine!' said my mum. 'Look at that! Aren't you a lucky wee girl – oh that's lovely that is, lovely!'

Everyone agreed. They all said how lucky I was and how generous Granny Matthew was. I felt as if I was looking at something else completely – it was horrible! However, maybe I should have been grateful because it was the only thing other than a bruise I could remember her ever gifting me. I was meant to fall over myself with happiness. I was told how delighted I would be to push this contraption around the streets of Dundee. Not only was it the first and only thing Granny Matthew ever gave me, it was the first thing I remember ever receiving at all. But it didn't seem particularly wonderful to me. It came from someone who hated me, and whom I now hated as a result. It wasn't a pretty little thing for dollies – and I didn't have any dollies to put in it anyway.

Once everyone had duly told Granny that she was the most generous woman in the world and that I was the luckiest girl in the street, the great hulking thing was taken outside and the door was closed behind me. Three years old and with a huge Silver Cross coach-built pram in front of me. I knew exactly what to do. Little triumphs would become my way of dealing with many of the unfair hands life dealt, and this would be my first. I would retaliate and I would make sure everyone knew just what I thought of Granny Matthew and her present.

The streets were busy, even though there weren't many cars, partly because of the horses that still went up and down, doing deliveries and collections for milkmen, coalmen and rag-and-bone men. I went a few roads away from where we lived – we stayed very close to my gran – and spent hours filling that infernal pram with every bit of mud I could get my hands on. I got the dirt from the gutters and the sludge from every little nook and cranny, and packed the Silver Cross as tightly as I could. I knew that Granny Matthew hated me, but I hated her, too, and this would be my way of showing her and everyone else just what I thought of the old witch. I remembered that Dad had been working on a building site near to our flat, so I even pushed the now incredibly heavy pram there to get even more detritus. There was plenty of it.

I stood back and looked at it when I was done. Plenty of people had walked past while I was busy, and they must have wondered what I was up to. No one asked. I saw a few of them smile at the little girl with the big project, but I don't think they would have guessed for a second what I was really up to. No doubt the passers-by thought it was cute or cheeky to see such a tiny wee thing busy loading muck and rocks into a filthy old pram.

For a little girl, it was quite an achievement. I can actually still remember feeling really proud. It was a glorious moment. I was rejecting what she had given me, which I particularly didn't want because such a fuss had been made of it. I somehow managed to get it back to her house, pushing it some parts of the way, dragging it others, even walking backwards when I had to. I rang her bell and waited. When she saw me standing there with her present completely ruined, her face was like thunder. The pram was left in the street. She never hit me, but she swore and shouted and near pulled my arm from the socket as she dragged me away. I think she was so furious that if she'd hit me, she'd have killed me. It was a pretty scary moment but powerful for me, too, because I had generated that response. So often things were done to me – I was hit or shouted at or starved – but, this time, I had created that reaction and that, in itself, was something I took some pride in.

Everyone else had gone back home by then, as I had been busy for so long, so she dragged me back to my mum, ranting and raving. I was called all the names under the sun, an ungrateful little besom, a horrible little girl, but I didn't care. No one blinked an eye about me getting hit; plenty of our neighbours saw her response but, to be honest, they would have thought I deserved it after such a 'terrible' thing. Afterwards, the whole family – and anyone else who would listen – got told about it and it was used as proof that I was a bad child.

But I knew that she hadn't given the pram to me because she liked me or cared for me or loved me. I knew she didn't feel any of those things so I didn't want anything to do with her. Of course, I got a hiding, but I was still very pleased with myself.

'You're such a bad little girl!' shouted Mum as she walloped me. 'You're evil! You're ungrateful! You're a complete waste of space! I have no idea what to do with you – you are such a bother to me, Lorraine. Really – what did I do to deserve you?' This was one of her favourite phrases, as was the next one which she said a lot: 'I'll beat the badness out of you, so help me, God, I will. Christ, I wish you'd never been born!'

On any given day, I'd be told that I was horrible, that she hated me, and that she wished I had never been born. The only thing I could cling on to was that, for once, they weren't the only ones doing the hurting; I had hurt them, too. It was my actions this time that had bothered them.

I didn't know it then, but the symbolism of what I had done with the pram was very important to me. I had been getting battered for so long and for no reason (not that any reason is ever valid) that I expected violence and a complete lack of positive emotion from my mother. This was a small way of showing that they couldn't expect me to react in the way they wanted. They treated me so badly and yet assumed that I would be delighted by a meaningless, tatty gift, when all it said to me, again, was that I was worthless. I hated the pressure on me to act in a particular way when it would have been totally fraudulent of me to do so. So I'd rebelled. And it was a shock to them.

Mum's everyday attitude to me was compounded by that of my gran and by my dad's coldness. He was always distant, he never engaged with anyone, really. I don't know why this was. He worked, he had a bit of fun with other people when he went to the pub or the bookies, and I know that he and Mum enjoyed being together sometimes. They loved to dance and would go out when they could, happy and bright. They were into their ballroom dancing and were both singers, often combining the two hobbies by going somewhere they could sing and dance for the evening. They were well known as singers, too. People made their own entertainment back then – all music in pubs and clubs was live, so there was always somewhere for them to sing. Dad would put on his best Sunday suit and Mum would dress up to the nines, with perfect make-up, jewellery, a little hat and gleaming dancing shoes with high heels. The ballroom dancing clubs they went to always made them happy and, later in life, they became members of working men's clubs, as well.

They did have a tempestuous marriage, largely because of Mum's moods, but amazingly they stayed together until her death many years later. My mum was violent towards him, too, although he never retaliated. Dad would wind her up until she started throwing things at him, screaming like a banshee. She'd smash her new plates over his head, throw his dinner at him. She'd call him names and put him down. He would disappear and return with flowers, they'd make up and be fine for a while, and then the cycle would start all over again. He'd buy her gifts and she'd be openly loving towards him, cook romantic dinners, dance to the radio, and generally seem quite content – for a while. When I was about three, they got a wind-up gramophone and they'd play records while they danced around the room. They were into Elvis, Sinatra, the Everly Brothers and Al Jolson. So they were both capable of happiness.

When I got much older, I identified with my father in many ways, but when I was little, he was just another adult who was emotionally stunted. Dad's whole focus was my mother. With me he was distant. He just didn't seem to be able, or want, to engage. He never played with me or cuddled me. He never threw me up in the air or swung me round by my arms. If Mum ranted about me being evil or naughty, he would just accept it. He never challenged her. He never questioned why she thought a three-year-old was like that, or even how I possibly could be. If she told him she'd had a terrible day with me, that I had been lazy, defiant and sullen, and that he needed to punish me, he did. If she told him to hit me, he did. When I was very little, Dad would spank me with his hand, but when I got older, he would use a belt or a slipper. The belt would be the one that held his trousers up and he would dramatically take it off to show how serious things were. There was something about being humiliated and hurt, and hit without anger or feeling, which stays with me to this day. It seemed like his job or his duty to hurt me because of my failures – failures that were created and reported by my mother.

I've often wondered why he did it without question. I think he loved my mother and maybe he just didn't know much about kids. He was a hard-working man who wanted a quiet life and she was easier to agree with than disagree with. Of course, he could have said 'no', he could have challenged her, but he never seemed to have the impetus to do anything. He just wanted to live his own life as quietly as possible. I do feel that he should have been man enough to stand up to her as, in my mind, she was a bully and she bullied him, too. In some ways, he was a victim as well, but he was an adult, and I was just a little girl; with the best will in the world, I can't justify what he did by ignoring my mother's violence and colluding in it. As an adult, he should have taken a stand. Instead he seemed almost to admire her temper. He was completely at her beck and call. She was the boss in every way. She wore the trousers and made all decisions. She controlled the finances, home, kids, everything, and his decision and choice to opt out of practically everything to do with his own family did, I'm sure, have consequences when I was in danger. If he had noticed more, if he had engaged more, perhaps things would have been different.

I remember one occasion when I was about three years

old and we were in the kitchen part of the house together. Mum and Dad were larking about, dancing with each other, cuddling and singing. I could see them quite easily as the house was so small. I was sitting on the worktop and I reached over to get something but fell.

'What are you doing now?' Mum shouted. 'Can I never get a minute to enjoy myself without you ruining it?'

I had fallen to the floor and was bleeding from my knees. I wasn't crying, I don't really remember ever crying, but it was sore and all I wanted was for her to pick me up and cuddle me.

'Look at that!' she shrieked, but not at me, not at my injuries. 'There's blood all over my clean floor!' She stared at me, shaking her head as if I'd done it on purpose. 'Right, that's it; I've had enough of you. Get to your bed this instant – and don't expect any bloody supper!'

So off I went. No cuddle, no supper, not even a wet cloth for my cut knees. I once tried to cuddle Mum. Stupid! She shouted at me to get off her, accused me of attacking her and hit me. So, for me, there was to be no affection, no fun.

I know there will be people reading this who find it hard to believe, but that's because they're good people and they find it natural to be affectionate towards their kids. It's hard, and it's painful, to recognise this simply doesn't exist for a lot of children, and I was one of them. Seeing affection between my parents and between other people outside the family let me know that it existed but it was denied to me.

I was too young to understand what was really going on, too young to know that what I was being denied had nothing to do with how I was — how could it have been down to me when I was only a little girl? I thought that I was the problem. After all, it was me who had never been taken in someone's arms and hugged.

I was a lost child.

CHAPTER 2

MY SAVIOUR

I won't grow tall and be like you.
I can't stay small and be like me.
I won't stay here, I'll disappear;
If I don't die.

I spent a lot of time on my own. Actually, I spent most of my time on my own. George was in hospital, Dad worked, Mum sometimes did a bit of time in a shop or something like that if the mood took her (and when she didn't, she made it clear that she didn't want me anywhere near her), and so I played in the gutter amid the grass and the mud. I helped in the steamie, and I spent a great deal of time lying on my back in the grass getting lost in the clouds. I lived in my own mind and invented imaginary friends. Even when I was very young, all the stories I wrote in my head had happy endings.

By the time I was four, I was becoming more aware of my life and what it entailed, just as any child does as they develop. A typical day for me would involve getting up and putting away the bed and bedding. I had to clean and lay the fire and do whatever chores I was given. This might earn me a 'piece' (a sandwich) if I was lucky. Then I'd go outside to play or to the steamie when it was cold. I would be outside most of the day unless my mum needed me to do something. They were different times and children were frequently left to their own devices, but I was undeniably a child whose basic needs were not being met. Such a child is a neglected child but this is a hard thing for anyone to notice as the absence of something is not easily spotted. People might notice a bruise but not the lack of a cuddle. Back then, even the bruises weren't an issue. It really was OK for parents to hit their children. My mum went too far, perhaps, but no one was looking anyway.

Until I was four, every day was the same, or, at least, it seemed that way – Mum hit me, battered me really, and Dad ignored me. I don't know if it was actually every day; I just know it was a lot.

As a four-year-old, I would sometimes chase after Dad when he was leaving for work, or if he was just trying to go about his business. I had no pyjamas or slippers, I slept in my clothes, so when I heard him leave for work in the morning, there were times when I chased him down the street at his heels. I could never catch up. My legs were too small, too short and too slow. I would try to engage him, try to get some healthy attention from him, but it never happened. I suppose I thought that maybe I had more of a chance with him. It seemed as if Mum's hatred of me could never be changed, but perhaps I could chip away at my dad's distance and coldness. I couldn't. I never did manage it.

Mum was red-haired, a fiery woman from Irish origins – a fact she used to excuse and explain her violence on many occasions. In fact, she often boasted about how she wasn't in control of her heart or her fists. That didn't seem fair or true to me. She always appeared to know exactly what she was doing when she hit me, but she continually claimed she had very little command over herself. She certainly got angry a lot and would always lash out. I didn't know her side of the family very well, but I was told that they were from a very poor background. I knew my maternal grandmother a bit, but Mum always made out that there was a story there which explained how she was. She would say, 'If you knew the life I had …' but the sentence was never finished, the story never told, before she walloped me another time, in memory of whatever she had been through.

From the earliest days I can recall, there was no joy for me in being a child. All I looked forward to was being alone and sitting, playing in a gutter. I would build things, throw things and try to hit other things. I found a marble once that became part of my treasure. Treasure was really anything that I came across. There were lots of kids playing in the streets and adults would sometimes engage with them, but mostly they were left to their own devices unless they were getting up to mischief.

For my part, I was quiet and didn't engage with people. Perhaps there were occasions when people talked to me but

I don't remember any and I know that I wouldn't have talked back to them.

Although I didn't often see my other grandparents or uncles (my mum's brothers), they weren't complete strangers and, when I did have contact with them, they treated me well. They were totally different to what I was used to. They were not 'huggy' and I barely knew them, but they spoke kindly and seemed to like me.

There was an ice cream parlour opposite our house run by Italians, and I would watch other kids come out with their treats, desperately hoping that they would drop them and I would be quick enough to scrape up what was left on the pavement before a stray dog got it. If wishing could ever make things happen, I'd have eaten a dozen ice creams a day! The shop was bright yellow and red, with a pull-down, striped shade to prevent the summer rays melting the stock. I do remember a time on a hot summer day when the large Italian lady who owned the shop handed me an ice cream. That cone never got a chance to drip even a drop! Like most women at the time she wore a large, full-length pinny and she had such a friendly face. She spoke to me in Italian and had a kind voice. I still love Italians – probably because of this! There were no fancy cones back then, so the fanciest thing about it all was that they had several flavours and wee sweets that they sprinkled over the top, called hundreds and thousands.

I was so hungry that I would pick anything off the ground to munch on, no matter how small or how dirty. I'd eat things which others had spat out. I would even collect used chewing gum off the pavement and desperately try to get some flavour out of it. I'd scrape things up which had been trodden on. There was nothing I would pass up if I thought I could eat it, as my stomach was always rumbling. This was the consequence of neglect not poverty. There was just never any food in the house and there certainly was never anyone bothering to ensure that I was fed.

Soup and bread and porridge were the main foods back then. I would sometimes scrape the porridge which had been made for Dad from the pot and eat it cold. Sometimes my mum would leave a bowl out, sometimes she wouldn't. A big pot of soup would be for the week and white bread was a staple. At times, I would get a 'piece' for tea with a scraping of lard and a sprinkle of sugar. The lard was replaced by Echo margarine in the late 1950s, which was a real step up in the world! If soup was made with a bone, ribs or some such, my dad got the meat and I would get the bones to suck on. My parents ate early and late, and I think Mum often just forgot about me, infrequently putting a piece of bread or soup down. There was also tripe and hough, occasionally but not often.

Meals were not as regular back then as they are now, and cupboards weren't full of snacks to graze on between meals – people often lived hand to mouth. There were occasions when no one ate, including my parents. There was no fruit except local berries. Strangely there was plenty of milk (only in bottles) so it must have been cheap. There were no fridges or freezers, though, so milk would be used to make puddings and old bread into bread pudding.

You might wonder why I didn't tell anyone about not being fed – but why would I? Lots of people were hungry and I personally did not feel aggrieved about it. It was just how it was and I was always very grateful for the food I got at the time. It's only looking back that I see the problem.

As time went on, Mum got slightly better at having some food around – but it was for everyone else and not me. I would always have to fend for myself. When my brother was home from hospital, there was more food around, and neither of my parents ever went short. When more siblings arrived, they always had access to food as well, but it remained a way in which my mother could control me even when it was in ready supply for everyone else.

The lack of food was definitely a theme of my childhood and Mum would add insult to injury by telling me how fat I was. Mum was obsessed by her own weight. She was overweight herself and on a permanent diet. I knew how many calories were in everything before I began school. When I did get soup or bread or something, I would eat it in a flash.

'Look at you!' she'd say. 'You're fat already and you're going to get fatter. Look at that stomach of yours!'

The truth was, I was skinny as a rake.

'I don't want you having the problems I've had, you hear me, Lorraine? Stop wolfing it down and stop eating so much, you greedy wee pig.'

When I did start school, I got free dinners and there was free milk, too, but it just meant that at home Mum could say that I'd been fed in school so she didn't need to give me tea. I often got into trouble for stealing food from school at lunchtime. When that was reported to her, it seemed to prove to her how greedy I was. I believed her. I believed I was fat. In fact, I believed her for years until I saw photographs which showed what a skinny, malnourished little thing I was.

Like many survivors, I still have issues around eating and around food. Some of that comes from what would happen to me later and the horrific tortures I suffered around eating, but some of it also came from my home life. The hunger and despair and sadness and loneliness and neglect and a hundred other things were so entangled that I honestly couldn't say which made my early years worse. It was all horrible.

That was my life.

That was my reality.

I didn't know how to be like other kids. I never learned how to play. I was always starving, ignored and cold.

I was conditioned to being unloved.

And then, as if by a miracle, everything changed. I'd been told about miracles. I'd listened to stories about them at Sunday school. We always went to church on the Sabbath. It was what most people did. We had special clothes for Sunday and everyone cleaned up, including me. You put your best clothes on, including a hat or headscarf. I liked it because there was always juice and biscuits and kind, softly spoken people there. The stories were of love and kindness and I adored all of it, from the baby Jesus being born to the Bible stories. I loved the tales of Daniel in the lion's den, and David and Goliath. Winning against the odds was my favourite theme. I loved the hymns and the kids' songs like 'Soldiers of the Lord', 'Jesus Loves Us', all that kind of thing. I loved the building, too, with its huge spire, big, arched, red doors, beautiful stained-glass windows, and an overwhelming sense of peace. I loved the sound of the organ and the smell of the place. I was a total believer.

I knew that Jesus loved children. I sometimes wondered if He loved me, if He would make a miracle happen for me, but I didn't dwell on it because that would take optimism, and I had none of that. I was a child who lived day to day, like most kids that age. I believed that Jesus loved all children but felt maybe I was not good enough. I believed in His miracles because that was what I was taught, but I was never sure if I would be worthy of one. But it happened anyway. The miracle came looking for me, and it found me.

My dad's family lived nearby and he had brothers. They were a close-knit, noisy family, and they were always around; apart from my Uncle Andrew. He was different because he had, what seemed to me, a very glamorous life. He was in the Army, which meant he was often away from Dundee, doing things I had no idea of, but that was what appealed. There was always talk of 'our Andrew' and 'our Andrew's in the Army, of course', but no details. I later discovered that he had a very humdrum career, but that was irrelevant in those days. He had left Dundee. He had made something of himself in everyone's eyes. He defended our country through choice. He wasn't forced to go, he chose.

And when Andrew came back on leave, the world changed.

I hadn't been too aware of him when I was a baby or a toddler. I was probably put into my bed when he visited and everyone celebrated but, one time, when he was on leave, I was there. I was in our house when Andrew rang the bell and I was there to see the magic that was brought about simply by his presence.

He was the golden boy. Dad was the eldest, Andrew the youngest. There was another brother in between them, and a sister – and what they all had in common, what the whole family agreed on, was that Andrew was wonderful. He was the one everyone loved. When Andrew walked in the room, there wasn't a soul who didn't notice; he generated happiness and laughter. He was very charismatic, charming and sociable. Though not a big man, he was handsome and had presence. He had an engaging laugh and, also, because he was a military man, there was a huge respect for him. It was not that long after the war. He was light-hearted with lots of new and up-to-date humour. His laugh was infectious, and he used it easily and often because he was such a lovely man. When Andrew arrived, there was music all the time and he was at the heart of it. His favourite song was 'Bless This House', and the irony of the words has never left me – 'Bless this house, O Lord we pray, keep it safe by night and day'. Andrew needed no instrument to make music; his voice was pure and pretty amazing on its own.

It didn't matter where we were, our house or someone else's when I got older, when Uncle Andrew came back, there would be parties and food and a great time. When we lived in that first house, people would be in and out all the time when Andrew was there, always ready for a party. They'd just leave their kids in their beds when they went out, it was all very casual. This potential for a party to happen at any moment was wonderful, but the most wonderful thing of all was that the man who caused all of this happiness loved me. He truly loved me. His love was like rain falling on the desert. I was so lacking in love and affection that as soon as someone showed a real interest in me, I soaked it up and could not get enough. I fell hook, line and sinker. My need was so great and Andrew filled the vacuum. He would bring me marbles, small trinkets, cuddly toys, presents. He would give me sweets. He would cuddle me and make me laugh. He gave me more attention in one visit than I had ever had in my life. Now that I was four, now that I was old enough to be around when Andrew was there, I thought I was the luckiest girl in the world. I was finally happy. He seemed always to have time for me, he always noticed me. In his eyes, I wasn't a horrible, unloved, nasty little girl – I was someone he wanted to spend time with, and I wanted to spend all of my time with him.

Often I would overhear that he was coming and I would see Mum cleaning more. I would wait outside, watching the street for him. I was not demonstrative so I wouldn't run to him but I would wait in the hope he might notice me. I didn't ever really trust that he would keep loving me but, amazingly, he always noticed me and always spoke directly to me, using nice words and telling me comforting things.

I was a child who had been taught to accept that life was

hard and joyless, and yet here was someone who was linked to me through blood and who actually liked me. Who loved me!

I would have done anything for him.

And I did.

The only time I was ever loved, the only time I ever felt that someone cared for me was when I was with him.

My Uncle Andrew. My saviour.

CHAPTER 3

DON'T MOVE

I'll never cry and won't forget
Being too small,
Surrounded by big bad wolves
called adults.

When people read or hear about child abuse, they often have no experience of it. Or, they think they don't. As an adult, as a survivor of abuse, and as someone who works with other survivors every day of her life, I can tell you now that you will know someone. Every person reading this book will know someone who has been abused – and you will probably also know an abuser.

Good people are horrified by what is done to children like me; but, sometimes, they don't see the whole picture. Paedophiles don't look any different from non-paedophiles. They don't have 'EVIL' tattooed on their foreheads. They mix with others, they can be teachers and shop assistants and doctors and carers. They can be everyone and anyone. If you think about it, if you think of the many books written by people like me, there's generally a common message and it isn't always about the abuser. It's about society, it's about those who could have helped but who didn't see what was happening, or who didn't want to see what was happening. That is what abusers prey on. They find the children who are lost or lonely, who can be groomed and exploited, and they know that there is no one looking out for those children because they have been labelled as 'difficult' or 'trouble'.

I was all of those things before my Uncle Andrew came onto the scene. I was unloved and badly treated, emotionally neglected and disliked. But I wasn't born cold and 'strange'. I was made that way by a mother who despised me and a father who never got involved in my care.

I never questioned that part of my life while I lived it. It was only once I left home that I began to try and work out what the adults were about and what their impact had been on me. My father had always left childcare to my mum. The gender roles were very clear and fixed. There was women's work – cleaning, cooking, sewing, mending, childcare, nursing – and men did what they considered 'men's stuff', like bricklaying, labouring, driving, and suchlike. Even the clothes were gendered and women and girls did not wear trousers. Working-class men had their roles to play, just as women did, and the fathers I knew didn't get involved in childcare.

Meanwhile, I was my mum's scapegoat. She told everyone that I was a horrible little girl. Her main tactic with Dad was to say how exhausted and worn out she was with looking after me, especially as I got older and began to get into 'bother'. She was a martyr who was trying to raise a challenging child. She would say it in shops, to neighbours, and to friends. I was a sullen kid and people were more likely to listen to adults than wonder whether I had a reason for being so reserved. She was believed. The stories went round my family about what a difficult child I was and they felt sorry for my mum. I would be lectured at every opportunity on good manners and good behaviour, and told that I should be helping Mum and not hindering her.

Within that family dynamic was Uncle Andrew.

A good man.

An Army man.

A man loved by his family.

A pillar of the community.

He didn't look dirty or smelly, he didn't act in a suspicious way. In fact, he was cleaner and kinder and nicer than everyone else. He was the only one I got love from. As a child, when Andrew was in my world, my days were lighter and happier.

If you have nothing, you cling on to anything. If someone gives a neglected and unloved child even a scrap of what they have never had, that child sees that scrap and grabs hold of it – even when it comes at a terrible, terrible price. I had never been loved. I had never even imagined I could be loved. I had never been told I was pretty. No one had ever said they wanted to spend time with me. No one had ever played with me. No one had ever made me laugh.

But then there was Uncle Andrew.

He did everything a good adult should – and the fact that he would then do everything a good adult should not wasn't in the picture at that stage. I loved him. You can't switch that love off when it doesn't come from anywhere else. Abusers prey on children like me. They are predators and they sense weakness, loneliness or neediness. They give us something and we need it desperately. When they then touch and hurt and abuse, those are actually things that many children are used to anyway. These things are the norm; it's the love which is unusual, and it's the love you'll do anything to keep.

Abusers are very good at finding children like me.

When I was about four, we moved house to a newly built council estate on the edge of town. Because of the expanding population after the Second World War there was a need to throw up housing estates as quickly and as cheaply as possible. This was one of those estates. The house was on the top floor of a new tenement which sat near the rise of a hill with rows of other tenements on either side. The road was wide with pavements. There was a car park but there were no cars parked for the first few years simply because no one had one.

We had a patch to grow our own vegetables and a back 'green' (a shared garden area) to hang up washing. The close was wide and clean with cream and yellow walls. The coal bunker was on the left side and the coal man could just tip the coal in from the stairwell so that the coal dust never got in.

The flat had a long 'lobby' (or hallway) which led to the living room, and the kitchen was a room off the living room. As you went in, there was a small bedroom facing you. Turning to walk down the lobby, on the left was a double bedroom and then, most amazingly, an indoor bathroom! This had a toilet, a sink, and even a built-in bath. On the right, there was another double bedroom. The kitchen was small by today's standards, with two deep stone sinks, one of them covered by a wooden board which could be removed for doing the clothes washing. There was a hand mangle between the sinks for squeezing the water out of the clothes and a built-in cupboard near the window which looked out over the 'backies' (the back gardens).

The living room was large and rectangular. There was a coal fire and here, too, the coal fire could heat up the water through a back boiler, which seemed a very modern contraption! There was a really big steel-framed window with small rectangular panes facing out onto the street with a good view of the estate.

The small bedroom had a built-in wardrobe but was only big enough for a single bed and nothing else. That became my bedroom. Furnishings were sparse at first, as it took time for my parents to fill such a large house. There was lino on the floors initially and then we progressed to rugs. There was only paint on the walls to begin with, but we soon used cheap lining paper and eventually proper wallpaper. And again we had a coin-operated electric meter.

We were still in Dundee, but this bigger place was

closer to my maternal granny. This was also the time that Mum gave birth to my little brother. I knew my mum was fat, but she'd always been fat, so I never thought she was having a baby. She disappeared for a few days and reappeared with my brother. He was pretty ugly and I had no interest in him at all. No one told me anything about the baby but I think that was how it was done back then. The only thing I remember being told was that this was my new brother, Donald, and I had to help look after him. I remember he cried a lot, especially at night, and he got fed with a bottle. No one breast fed as that was seen as disgusting – it was actually considered aspirational to bottle feed, unlike now when there is more of a middle-class tendency to do the opposite. There was free government milk for babies that came in big, round, white tins and I have a clear memory of those around the house when Donald came along.

George remained in hospital for most of this period. I don't ever remember being taken to visit him and, on the rare occasions when he came home, I was told to keep quiet and stay away from him. As a result, I didn't really have any relationship with him at all. I didn't have much to do with Donald either. I used to watch as Mum hugged him and kissed him and sang songs to him.

With the baby, and with George when he was home, Mum was gentle and caring. She would rock Donald and smile and play with him. I learned lots of nursery rhymes and baby songs through watching her with him. Mum had a tin bath that she would bathe Donald in. She'd sit it in front of the fire and fill it from the kettle, check to make sure it was not too hot, and gently bathe him. It was nice to watch. I looked at how she was with my brothers and saw a different woman. The problem was me. I was such a vile child that she couldn't love me.

'Look how cute he is!' she'd say to me. 'Why can't you be like that? Look how much he smiles! Why do you never smile?'

It was constant.

'He's not greedy. See that? He's had enough for now; he's not guzzling it, like you do with food. He knows when to stop.'

Having a new baby, a boy who was healthy and who smiled, made the contrast with me even greater.

'He's smiling at me again!' she'd laugh. 'Ah, you love your mummy, don't you wee Donald?' Then she'd glare at me and sigh the sigh of the long-suffering parent.

She was capable of being a nice mum, I could see that. She'd managed it with two other children, so I must have something rotten in me that stopped her being that way with her only daughter.

There had been a lot of excitement when we had packed up for the new house, but I don't remember thinking that my life would change that much. My parents were very happy, indeed, as it was a big step up. Everyone in the old close was talking about the move and congratulating them. Boxes and bags were everywhere. In those days, most moves were moonlight flits as people left debts behind but our move was upfront and everyone knew about it. There were lots of trips on the bus to the new house carrying stuff, and my dad's work lorry also took some things there for us.

Moving did mean a few changes in my life, however, and one of them was the start of nursery.

I lasted a week.

There was no excitement to that, no build-up to my attendance. Lots of children count down the days until they start at playgroup or nursery, but I had none of that. I was just told, on the morning, that I'd be going. I washed myself and got dressed. When we arrived, after having walked there in silence, the place was already full of other kids. There was a smell like old boiled eggs. I didn't like it. There were low down hooks for coats all in a row with little face cloths hanging from them. It was nothing like nurseries today. The staff wore overalls and everything was in rows. Lots of children were sitting on small seats and at small desks playing quietly with a variety of things. It was quiet and orderly. Children were much quieter back then in general – adults were in charge and children knew it. It was in a church community hall, I think, and run to almost military discipline. Mum took me to the door and said, 'You'll stay here. I'll be back later. Don't move.'

That was it.

She was gone.

There was no cuddle or kiss, no wish that I'd have a nice day or promise to be back soon. I suppose she would know that I wouldn't miss her anyway, so there was no touching scene of me shedding a tear as my lovely mummy walked away. I stood there, watching more children come in, and felt absolutely clueless.

I didn't know how to play with the others.

I didn't know how to interact. I didn't know what to say or do. One of the nursery teachers came over to me and smiled.

'Hello,' she said. 'Have you come to play with us today?'

I said nothing. I didn't trust anyone and I knew – or thought I knew – that no one liked me. I was a horrible girl; ugly and nasty, selfish and terrible. I knew all of this because it was always being said to me. I didn't make eye contact with her; I just stared at the floor.

The woman walked away after trying to get me to talk for a few minutes and then returned with another woman. Again, they tried to draw me out. One of them touched my arm. She was being kind, as I must have looked a poor wee thing standing in my tatty clothes, with not a hint of a smile on my face. I pulled away.

I only had one thing to hold on to. My mum had only given me one instruction – stay there, don't move. That was what she had said and that was what I would do. It was defiance, but that defiance came from fear and confusion. I was a four-year-old child who didn't know how to play. Nursery was a completely alien world to me, so I clung on to the command – stay there, don't move – and promised myself that I would shame Mum by doing that and that alone. I knew what I was doing.

Throughout the rest of the play session, people came up

to me and tried to talk. There were lots of different approaches; some would laugh and ask why I was being so silly, some would get a bit cross and say they'd had quite enough of my behaviour, some of them would even try to drag me away. It made no odds to me.

When Mum came back, hours later, I was standing in the same spot. I hadn't taken my coat off. I hadn't gone to the toilet. I hadn't spoken. It went on for the whole week. Every day I did the same. Mum didn't care what I did. I wasn't showing her up (which she would have cared about – a lot), I was being quiet and odd, which she already thought I was anyway. All it really did was show her that she was right about me all along.

'Couldn't even manage nursery school! Stupid child!' was her response to anyone who asked.

She was told not to bring me back. I was strange. Not like the others. But I had never learned to play – that would have involved me interacting in a normal way with other people. I was scared and completely out of my depth. There were so many kids and so much going on; I was completely bewildered so held on to the one thing Mum had told me. It should have been an opportunity, though, for someone else to look at the neglected little girl and see that something wasn't right, that something wasn't fitting. I was tiny and I was odd. Why didn't that seem worthy of investigation? I kept my head down. I didn't make eye contact. I wouldn't move. When forced to move, I moved woodenly. I kept quiet. I tried not to draw attention to myself, not realising that that in itself brought me more attention.

Don't Move

What had already been done to me in terms of emotional neglect and physical cruelty had made its mark. I was isolated and lonely. I didn't know how to engage with others, adults or children. I didn't trust anyone, certainly not adults; I had no sense that they were there to look after me or protect me.

I was alone.

CHAPTER 4

SUCH A GOOD WEE GIRL

I won't grow old.
Adults hurt you
Make you cold.

It was at this time in my life when my Uncle Andrew made his mark, as he was around a lot more once we moved house. Through being in the Army, he had travelled a lot. This was seen as unusual in my childhood, people didn't go on foreign holidays at the drop of a hat, and most people in my world didn't even have passports. Andrew's foreign trips brought a whiff of exotic adventure. Again, there were no details; it was enough to hear that 'Andrew was away' to get a sense of awe. I suppose that his absences also made the heart grow fonder for everyone. When he came back, it was a novelty. The rest of the family saw each other all the time, with the various niggles and petty disagreements which come from relatives living too close together in poverty. When the youngest son returned with money and gifts, he was very much admired and celebrated.

At this point, he was unmarried and had no children. Without responsibilities, Andrew would sail back into my life every so often – into all our lives – with a smile and a song. He would sing Elvis songs – 'Crying in the Chapel' was a favourite for a while, as were others, such as 'Take my Hand, Precious Lord'. He liked slow songs generally. He had a very flexible voice and could reach amazingly high notes.

Andrew was never too tired or cross or busy to play games. I was a child who didn't really know how to play so I never asked for his interaction, but that didn't matter. He was the one who initiated it, who sensed when I needed some attention (which was always, really), and who gave me his time. I'd never had that before, from anyone. I loved it when he visited. I loved the attention. I simply hadn't experienced any of what he brought before; it was a new way of living. I was a lot happier.

I would always know when he was back by the under-current of excitement around me. Mum cleaned more, Dad practised his latest Al Jolson number. And I came to life – for him. He played and I existed. Instead of being this invisible thing, always in the way, I became somebody. He was wonderful.

When Andrew arrived, everybody seemed to cheer up. There would be a party atmosphere all of the time because everyone adored him. He was charming – he still is. He was articulate, and he had the voice of an angel. When Andrew sang, everyone listened. It touched your soul. His voice was high and pure. My dad's side of the family can all sing, but Andrew took it to another level.

When he left, everything would go back to 'normal'. Horrible normality. Work resumed, there was less drinking and there were no parties. 'Normal' was everyday life. In the new house, 'normal' meant digging the vegetable plot and planting seeds and potatoes, it meant washing clothes and helping with the mending. And then, he would come back, and it would all be perfect again. It's hard to describe just how much he changed our lives. When Andrew was away with the Army, everything was dark and boring. My mother wavered between hitting me and ignoring me. Dad was in a world of his own. One brother was in hospital and the other was a boring baby. I had no friends, no family who cared. I was a lost little girl.

Then Andrew would return and it was as if light filled the air. I felt happy and excited and scared in case he did not remember me. I was anxious and thrilled at the same time. When he saw me, made eye contact with me, noticed me, it was overwhelming and quite hard to cope with.

Mum would laugh and sing, too. There would always be food on the table, and I wouldn't be slapped if I went anywhere near it. Parties would happen every night – or so it seemed to me. Even when they weren't planned, if Andrew was in the house, he would start singing, everyone would be happy, the drink would flow and a party would miraculously appear. No one ever joined in when he sang because it was so beautiful. He never sat down; he always stood, sang and held court. He was the centre of everything. It was a world of smiles and enjoyment.

And the most amazing thing of all was that the man who

was the cause of all this wonder noticed me. No matter how many people surrounded him, his eyes would seek me out and he would give me a little smile. When he sang, he would search the room with his gaze and make me feel as if he was dedicating the song to me. In a hundred tiny ways – a wink, a look, a grin, a word – he made me feel special and important.

Andrew loved everyone and spent time with everyone and was special to everyone. Yes, he was like that with me and I thought it was just me, but, actually, he was a real people person and everyone liked him. They would have thought nothing of him being nice to me because that was the type of guy he was.

Everyone wanted a piece of Andrew when he was on home leave, but we were the lucky ones. He stayed at our house a lot. He also played with me – a lot. I was four and only a little slip of a thing, half-starved and fully neglected, there was nothing of me.

'Come on, wee Lorraine,' he'd say to me, 'let's have a game of horsey.'

I was still unsure and expected the attention to disappear, so when my uncle came up with the idea, I loved it. 'Horsey' was his favourite game.

'Climb up onto my back then,' Uncle Andrew would tell me, as he kneeled down on the floor. 'Time to get up on your horsey.'

I'd clamber up, happy as a lord, and he'd neigh and gallop around the living room. It was always just us. Mum might be there, Dad might be there, but they would be doing other things, so Andrew and I would have the place to ourselves. When Dad was in, he would be reading newspapers but he wasn't often in at the same time as me, as he worked and then went to the pub. Mum would be busy cooking, cleaning, polishing, sewing, knitting or darning.

I don't know how often we had played that game before I started to notice things. I noticed that sometimes, when I slid off his back, his hand would slip in my knickers as he helped me down. I noticed that, a few times, when I climbed on, his fingers would touch my private parts. I noticed that when we played sitting-down horsey (with me on his lap, facing him), his hands and fingers were all over me, touching me, exploring me.

At the time it was only a game to me.

I saw nothing wrong with it.

I knew it happened, but that was it.

Andrew wasn't hurting me – not deliberately – and he was my favourite person in the whole world. These things were just part of playing horsey. Anyway, when it happened, he was always kind and he always had a gift for me, a sweet or a little toy. He was a good man, I thought. He was the best person I knew.

Sometimes, when I sat on his lap to play, his hands didn't just go into my knickers by accident. I knew that because he wasn't helping me to climb on or off the horse. I would just be sitting there, we'd be talking, and I'd feel him touching me, stroking me. Sometimes, he would tell me Bible stories while he did this.

When he stopped, he'd give me a cuddle.

'You're such a good wee girl, Lorraine,' he'd tell me, and then he'd make some noise to let others know we were having fun. We played when the room was full, too, but he never touched me on those occasions. The actual games would be the same, but the context would be different. The affection remained, but there would be no sexualisation to what was going on. It all looked perfectly innocent, perfectly harmless, no more than an indulgent uncle kindly taking the time to play with the difficult child in the family.

The grooming started so early, and he was very, very good at it.

Pretty much everything he did to me had a sexual element. He would sometimes do it when other people were there, because it was hidden. It would look as if he was just jiggling me about as I sat on his knee, but his hands would be inside my knickers. At that age I had no concept as to whether that was all right or not. I just didn't know. Even when he wasn't actually touching me, every action, every gesture was either about him touching me or preparing me to be touched, so it was still linked to the abuse. By teaching me to trust him and by giving me the love I got from no one else, he was letting me know – even if I didn't realise it – that there was a trade. He gave me gifts, I got touched. He gave me attention, I got touched. He hugged me, I got touched. He told me nice things, I got touched.

There were a lot of tickling games and chasing games, too, and there was always a sexual element to them as well. When he picked me up, his hands would be between my legs. They were never anywhere 'innocent'. They were always where he chose them to be. If he helped get me ready for bed, there would be touching and stroking of my private parts. At that age, I knew nothing. No one said anything, perhaps they saw nothing, but I had no idea. He would babysit a lot, and there were times when other adults would be in a different room; he always contrived some way of being there and some way of getting to me.

I remember walking down the street at one point when I was very little and he was holding my hand. I was delighted because no one had ever done that before and yet it is such a natural thing for a child to experience. When I saw him, my world changed. I wasn't a demonstrative child, I was reserved and subdued, but when I saw him, things would lift. He would come over, pick me up, and cuddle me. It was alien to me. I saw it happen to others, but never to me until Andrew came into my life. Of course, he must have been there before I start to remember things, common sense tells me that he was no doubt touching me from the earliest times, but my concrete memories begin from the age of three.

Pre-school, my recollection of him is of love and touching, fun and stroking, games and poking, comfort and rubbing. 'I love you so much,' he would tell me, and they were words I'd never heard before. 'You're a very special wee girl, do you know that?' I did. For those brief moments when he changed my world, I did know it and I believed it.

The rest of the time, I felt I was in the way, I was ugly and I was stupid. I was surrounded by negativity when he wasn't around. I could do nothing right, I was awkward, probably due to being left-handed in a right-handed world, but also due to low self-esteem. Andrew would appear and it would all change. As a very little kid, I suppose I craved it. The good bits, the comfort weren't linked with sexual, bad things at that age.

Did I scream?

Did I tell?

Did I stop going anywhere near him?

Of course I didn't.

He was all I had. Even if it had occurred to me that it was wrong, no one would have believed me, no one would have taken my side against Andrew. He was loved, I was not. Anyway, it never entered my head to tell. Not just because I had no one to tell and no one would have listened, but because he wasn't physically hurting me.

There will be a lot of things in my story which may make the reader feel uncomfortable or incredulous, and here is where they begin. Even for those of you who have been abused, you may never have heard anyone admit to this before, but I know, as someone who works with survivors, that it is one of the great unspoken secrets that many of us still carry – what Uncle Andrew did to me felt nice.

It felt nice to be touched and loved by the person who was, by far, the nicest adult in my life. He always did things to make me feel special, and this wasn't something which made me cry or left me bruised. One afternoon, it did hurt but, at that time, it seemed to me to be a one-off.

Mum was out and Dad was at work. Andrew and I were alone in the house – he was always a willing babysitter and my parents were always delighted to have me off their hands. There had been lots of messing about, and there was a great deal of tickling. Of course, now, as an adult and parent, I can see what he was doing and I'd be horrified if I saw anyone acting that way with a child, but to me, at four years old, it meant nothing. Andrew had touched me that day, and he had 'tickled' my private parts, but he went too far. He picked me up and put his fingers inside me, but he pushed harder than he usually did and it was sore. All I can remember is an instance of pain – I think he must have gone further than he intended.

I yelped, and he was instantly concerned.

'What is it? What's wrong?' he asked. 'Is something wrong?'

I wasn't sure what to say so muttered something about an ache. He would have known exactly what he had done. I recall lots of apologies – 'I'm so sorry, my poor wee Lorraine, silly Uncle Andrew!' – and then he cuddled me before going to his coat and giving me a handful of sweeties.

'There you go, there you go,' he said. 'Everything's fine. Everything's fine. It was an accident, it was an accident.'

And it was. He had apologised. No one else ever did that when they hurt me. It made me feel special – it was just another thing to make me feel special. I believed it was an accident, because people have accidents all of the time, and I had no conception that he was doing anything wrong to start with. I remember being slightly confused for a moment, because he had never hurt me before, but when he explained that it was an accident and he soothed me and comforted me, I understood. I couldn't work out why he was so agitated, but I reasoned that it was just because he thought I was in pain. No other reason came to me – how could it?

It was, however, the first time that it felt strange. It was the first time I thought, what was that? I had no way of thinking it through because I had to accept the adult explanation. But it had been a different type of pain, and it was his agitation which threw me. 'Are you all right? Are you all right?' he kept asking. 'Now, now, we'll just have a wee play, will we Lorraine? We'll just have a nice, quiet wee play. I didn't mean to hurt you, I really didn't. I'm so sorry, I'm so sorry.' I thought that was odd. No one usually bothered about how I felt, and Mum hurt me all the time without caring, so when he tried to quieten me down, I did wonder. He took me for sweets, and it was never mentioned again.

He was breaking me in, but I was completely oblivious to the fact. The getting hurt actually became a huge reward because I got lots of gifts and love and comfort and food from it. A little bit of pain didn't bother me. When Mum hurt me, there was nothing but shouting and bruises. When Andrew did, I could very well end up with a new dolly or some skipping ropes or a ball.

The showering of gifts after the early abuse was instant. He brought lots of things with him every time; he was stocking up on payments, which is an indication of how it was all thought out and planned. I had no idea that there was anything sexual to what he was doing. As a child, I simply didn't see it; it was just a combination of great love and accidental hurting.

My mum would hurt me and hit me, she wouldn't apologise and say 'sorry'; she meant to do it, she meant it to hurt and she would say it served me right. When Uncle Andrew accidentally hurt me, he was so sorry, he said he didn't mean it, he wanted to make it better. Quite often, he wanted to rub it better. From a child's perspective, this made everything he did look innocent.

For me, getting hurt by him was a good thing, because it meant I got more of everything that I craved, the love and attention more than the material things. As an adult I see the absolute horror of it all, but back then? I was just Uncle Andrew's good wee girl.

CHAPTER 5

DREAMING

I hate adults
Adults do not ever care
Adults tie you to a chair.
Hate you. Hurt you.

As was the case in many British cities in the late 1950s and early 1960s, there was a huge programme of house-building, and attempts to move people out of dirty, overcrowded inner-city areas. Things were changing rapidly. It seemed that every day there would be something new and our new home was a microcosm of what was happening in society. When we moved house, having a sink and bath inside and the indoor toilet were incredibly thrilling. I remember the excitement so well, although there were also comments about it not being hygienic to have a toilet inside where people lived! There was hot water for the first time and it will be hard for anyone young reading this to understand just what a treat — and a miracle — that was.

The trams began to disappear, as did the trains which

went into outlying areas. I had been on trams (slow and smelly and very uncomfortable), but they were gone by the time I started school. The rag-and-bone man with his horse and cart still came regularly down the street and children would swap their clothes for a balloon or a goldfish. I actually got a goldfish in a swap for my coat once but my mum put it down the toilet. I had a pretty cold winter that year, coatless – and without my goldfish. Women would sell him their rags in return for money and it was the most natural thing in the world, without any judgement on the part of others.

Onion Johnnies were common, too. They were Frenchmen on bikes with huge strings of onions which they sold in the streets. There would also be people selling whelks and mussels and crabs in the streets. They were sold live and you then cooked them yourself. The fisherman and milkman would also set up stalls in the streets – and they didn't just sell fish and milk either.

Bottles were always glass, never plastic, and you got money back on them; people kept jam jars, bottles and other glass to sell back to the shopkeepers. Even the lids off milk bottles were kept, washed and sold back.

Things were changing, though. Everyone talked about how wonderful modern times were. There were street lights now and, when I was about eight years old, we became the first family in our street to get a TV. It took four men to carry it up the stairs and the whole street turned out to watch. It was a huge wooden case with doors that opened out and folded back. In the centre of it was a tiny

TV screen. It even had a radio. It took ages to warm up and made a high-pitched whining noise as it did so. There would be a grey speckled screen that gradually became a hazy black, white and grey picture. The sound was poor but understandable. It was hired and operated by a coin. A sixpence, if I recall rightly. Kids were not allowed to watch it at first because there were rumours that it might be dangerous.

In electrical shops in town, TVs and radios and things like washing machines began to appear. Our first washing machine was a twin tub. Washing went in one side, which was filled with water through a hose attached to the tap, the water then heated up and it would swirl around for a while. Then you transferred the washing to the other side where you would attach another hose to empty it into the sink and it would spin. It was very noisy.

A lot of my memories of growing up are very vague when I think about what changed, but I think that's the same for everyone. There were so many new developments but they 'just happened' so they weren't charted as such in my life, they just started to appear. Television and household appliances were, of course, huge cultural shifts, but there were other things going on throughout my childhood which were even bigger, but, again, they 'just happened'. There was the war in Vietnam and the assassination of JFK, but there were also smaller changes such as those relating to fashion. When the 1960s kicked in, women began wearing more adventurous stuff. Trousers, shorts and slacks took off and the caps and hats started to disappear. It was all changing, but none of it really mattered to me – all that I cared about was Andrew.

I had a hunger for his attention. I craved love. I wanted hugs and he gave those things to me – but there was a price. Everyone always commented on how much he loved kids – and, in those days, there was nothing suspicious about that type of comment. The touching continued every time he was there, it just became part of the life I had with him. It would happen when we played games. It would happen if he came into my bedroom. It would happen if he tucked me into my bed at night. He would make a great fuss of straightening the bedclothes, of smoothing the sheets down, and then his hands would wander under those same sheets and he would feel the need to smooth my nightdress down, too. There was always the touching. It was part and parcel of who he was. It was all done in a completely non-threatening way.

I wasn't scared of Uncle Andrew; I was scared of my life without him.

In the same street as us, in the new area where we now lived, there was another man who had the same inclinations as Andrew, but not the same opportunities. This man – Sandy – may have been a distant family member, I'm not sure. Back then, every adult got called auntie or uncle by children if they were a friend of your parents, but I also have vague memories of Sandy being at some family events, so perhaps there was a blood link there, too.

I was still being ignored and left to my own devices by my parents. I preferred it that way to some extent, because if I was out of the house, hanging around the streets and looking for scraps to eat, at least I wasn't on the other end of Mum's fist. If Andrew wasn't there, I had no desire to be at home.

One day, while I was piling up stones on the pavement, Andrew appeared.

He chatted to me for a while before I asked, 'Are you going to our house, Uncle Andrew?'

'No, hen,' he said, 'I've got some business to attend to.' He looked up at the sky which was getting darker as rain threatened. 'You could do me a favour, though.'

I waited. I'd do anything for him.

'Can you go round to Uncle Sandy's for me?'

I nodded. 'What for?' I asked.

'Just tell him that Andrew sent you,' he smiled. 'Good girl.'

Sandy was charismatic, too – not in the same league as Andrew, but he was still a charming, friendly man. It was a small community and pretty well everyone knew everyone to some degree. He lived with his wife and three children in a tenement just like ours. When I got to Sandy's flat, he was the only one there.

I told him that Andrew had sent me and he smiled. 'Did he now? Did he now?' he asked. 'Well, Lorraine, what shall we do? Do you like playing? Your Uncle Andrew tells me that you do.'

I nodded. And that's what we did. We played games.

'I hear you like playing horsey,' said Sandy. 'Would you like a wee game of that?'

It seemed completely innocuous to me. The very idea of a grown man playing in a flat alone with a small girl didn't strike me as odd at all, given that the only person I ever played with was another grown man; so that's what we did. We played horsey. And did he touch me? Of course he did. I have no doubt that was exactly what I had been sent there for and I saw no reason to consider it abuse. Sandy wasn't as loving as Andrew when he stroked me and touched me, but he didn't hurt me. I was used to it; it was what I knew.

I wasn't a lovable, cuddly child – apart from with Andrew. I was more likely to push people away and I wasn't the easiest of children, but Andrew undoubtedly paved the way for Sandy's interaction with me. They must have colluded; I can see no reason to think otherwise.

Andrew's 'activities' continued, and so did Sandy's – but it was Andrew who clearly had the more direct access to me, even more so since the move.

Moving house had also allowed me to get to know Mum's side of the family a bit better as they were now, geographically, nearer to us, as the Council tended to put families close together if possible. So, around this time, I got to know my gran and really liked her. She was Irish, shouted a lot and smoked like a chimney, which is why she died of cancer some years later, no doubt. My granddad was more distant. He was an Englishman and a gifted musician. Mum had three brothers and none of them seemed terribly close to one another. Gran had a terrible temper and would throw things around, but never actually hurt people, as far as I could see. As I got older and she got sicker, I would go to the shops for her to buy her Wild Woodbine cigarettes and her wee dram (whisky), as children were allowed to buy these things over the counter without any problem. I would go with a note from her to the local grocer's, called Starkey's, and they would put the stuff in the bag without blinking an eye. She had a German shepherd dog which I began to walk for her, too.

Gran knew I was a troubled child and I know she argued with my mum about me because my mum forbade me from visiting her when I was about nine. I still managed to sneak round a few times, but she died when I was twelve.

Mum wasn't the sort of person who ever pretended to be something she wasn't, though. Her front of being a respectable mum was there, but only to some extent. Regardless of who was there, she would be angry and lash out whenever she felt like it, but this anger would be less likely to appear in the first place if we had visitors, as she was very sociable and lightened up a lot in the presence of others. Another bonus to having people around, in her eyes, was the possibility that they might entertain her horrible child. I was still a thorn in her side, as she never tired of telling me.

Mum was always different when other people were about. She became very hospitable and the good china would come out to be put on the good tablecloth. She laid out decent biscuits, not broken ones (not that I ever even got the broken ones!). She would change her voice according to who she was speaking to, as well. Even on the street she would have a posh voice for some people. I remember her saying things like, 'Oooh, Lorraine – look at the mess of your dress again! I despair of keeping you clean! I only changed you an hour ago!' There would be tinkling laughs between her and the other woman, as they would raise their eyebrows in knowing exasperation of being a mother with difficult children. It was all lies – she'd leave me to look filthy for weeks on end. Whenever I did something that wasn't quite right in her eyes, I'd catch a look and know that her fists would fly when everyone had left.

My mother was a tiny woman, less than five feet tall, with red curly hair. When she was younger, she was lovely look-ing – but I take after my father more. He is dark; I'm told there's some Egyptian blood in the family tree and I was certainly the butt of some ill-educated and nasty racist insults in my time. It was this, along with my mum's hatred of me, which pushed my thoughts in an imaginative direc-tion. When you're a child, you come up with lots of explanations for things which don't make sense to you, and I lived in my head most of the time anyway. Inside myself, I had all sorts of fantasies that all ended the same way – I convinced myself that she was not my real mother.

I had lots of things to back my notion up – I didn't have red hair like her, I didn't have pale skin like her. I could see that my dad was my dad but, the more I thought about it, she just couldn't be my mum.

One day, when I had been left at home on my own, I was

raking through things as kids do. I came across an old photograph album. To my delight, there were wedding photographs in it showing my dad as the groom – but a different woman as the bride. At last I had evidence! She wasn't my mum. I had another real one who would love me. I lived off that thought for weeks. I had an amazing secret which was mine alone.

I convinced myself that I was living with her because something had happened to my real mum and that was why this imposter hated me. This kept me going every time she hit me. I clung on to my knowledge that I had a real mum, a mum who really did care for me. Kids need that. They need hope. When I was battered and bruised, I would sneak off to their bedroom and open the cupboard, take out the old wedding album and stroke my real mum's face. In candle-light, I would think about how, if she was with me, she would love me and look after me and protect me.

It was inevitable that I would be caught out. When I was, I lost everything for a while. I had thought I was alone, but my so-called mum had come back home to collect something. When I heard her walk towards her room, I froze.

'What the fuck are you up to?' she snarled. She walked closer to me, a tiny little girl huddled in a corner with a wedding album stinking of damp. 'What have you been poking about in, you nosy little bastard?' she asked, as she snatched the book out of my hands. She shook her head and raised her fist. It was only when she had finished raining blows on me, that she told me the truth – laughing, she informed me that my dad had been married before he met her. His first wife had died within a year of their wedding. She couldn't have been my real mother after all.

The bruises hurt, but the loss of my fantasy was worse.

I had just started to read when I found an encyclopaedia which told me that, on the day of my birth, there had been a UFO sighting in Fife. It was close enough for me to weave a tale. I created a new fantasy in which aliens had come from outer space, landed in Dundee, and lost me, one of their children.

I was clever and practical and always had evidence to back these stories up. What I was clinging to with my imaginary lives was the notion that maybe there was a chance for me to get away from my life – a life which was so terribly damaging. I lived in hope that one day the aliens, or my real mum, would come and rescue me. These little triumphs and secrets kept me strong.

CHAPTER 6

STRONGER

I don't care
I'm not there.

The thing which kept me strongest was Andrew. His love for me was the only bright spark in my life. I didn't know how warped that love was, I only knew that he loved me. He never told me to keep quiet about what he was doing to me. Even as I got older and it began to dawn on me how wrong it all was, I would have defended him with my life because I loved him. It was a distorted love but it was love nonetheless. If anybody had tried to say something, or accuse him, I would have denied it.

Andrew was a good-looking guy, like one of those old film stars. He looked like a real gentleman, and everything was pressed and clean about him. He was absolutely immaculate, with even his hankies ironed. He was very precise, a proper military man. He was dashing, like a hero in a war film, and quite the mystery character because he would come and go.

Andrew always gave me lots of things, sometimes a penny (which was a lot for sweets in those days), and lots of treats. He brought balls and skipping ropes, not great huge things but there was always something. But he didn't need to bring anything for me – seeing him was a reward in itself, given how everyone was when he was there. He changed everything; the place lit up and so did I. It was just wonderful, like lots of Christmases at once.

We adored each other – or so I thought. I never suspected at all in those days that he had a plan, a reason for being so good to me. I felt rescued when he was around. People who know what happened to me say how awful it was, but what if he hadn't been there? Maybe I would never have had any decent attachment to a human being. Maybe I would never have loved anyone. I know that it sounds incredible that I now think that way, but I've been over my story so many times in my own head that I've considered everything.

I know now that research states that if you don't have a positive attachment before the age of three, it is unlikely you will ever effectively develop one. It is heartbreaking to think that mine was to a paedophile, but if I hadn't had that, perhaps I would have gone through my whole life not being able to form good relationships. Out of the dark did come light.

Andrew was gentle. He did not try to cause me pain (I don't know what he was like with others). He did hurt me, of course, but it wasn't violent abuse. If someone just hurts you, it's easier to feel anger and hatred and all of those other things that actually help you recover. But when you're trying to reconcile how you feel about non-violent abuse, it is so much harder for a child to work out. The mixed feelings of love and shame, and then when your body physically responds to the abuse, things get terribly messy.

I tried to work through that later on and it was horrible. In some ways, it was worse to have experienced the sort of abuse I did as it leads to such a twisted, distorted interpretation of love which lasts until adulthood. When you do eventually choose to make love with a partner and have a good feeling, it throws you back and you realise just how awful and disgusting everything else was. That pulls you and affects your present. Triggers can be good things as well as bad things, and that was one of the hardest lessons I've ever had to learn, trying to process what he did.

What he was doing was deliberate and vile – making a child love you to the extent that they will accept abuse is so calculated, particularly since a child doesn't know one thing from another.

From my earliest recollections, even bouncing on his knee as a little child, I was aware that there was something in his trousers. There were lumpy bits and one of our games was to see if we could grow 'it'. It would just be part of the game.

'Come on, then,' he'd say in a jolly fashion. 'Let's play one of our favourite games. Shall we see if we can grow it? Can you be a clever girl and make it bigger?' Once he did have an erection, it would be emphasised again – albeit in a subtle way – that this was all my doing. 'There we are! Look at what you've done! Look at what you've done to Uncle Andrew!' It was one of my favourite games, according to him, and similarly, according to him, it was entirely down to me that he had an erection.

He would laugh about it and he seemed really happy. It was made out to be silly, fun and games. As a child, it wasn't something threatening, it was just what we did. He was always clothed during those early days when it happened. If he got an erection when we were playing and he hadn't led up to it, he would say, 'Look! Look, Lorraine! It's there! Aren't you clever?' He would tell me how proud he was of me, and how amazed he was that I could do this thing so well.

Sometimes he would pretend it was magic. 'Aren't you clever?' he'd say. 'I don't know how you do that – it's your own special wee magic trick, isn't it?' I didn't know how I did it either. I didn't even know what it was for a while. Andrew would sometimes say, 'We won't tell anyone about that,' but he wasn't specifically telling me not to tell. There is a difference. He was making it all seem like our little secret, and also making it seem as if I was the driving force, given that I was the one who could do the magic. He tried to make it seem cheeky rather than bad or sinister.

Once we had moved to the second house, he had different opportunities. There was no inside toilet in the other flat, so there would have been no way to excuse his behaviour if he had ever been caught undressed or half-dressed. That all changed. Sometimes I would walk into the bathroom and he'd be there. He'd leave the door open and he would be standing there, not actually using the toilet, as he would have been facing away from me or sitting down, but clearly waiting for me to 'find' him with his pants down.

I know now that on the occasions when I found him doing 'something' in the bathroom, with the door conveniently unlocked, he was actually masturbating. I had no idea what that was when I first saw it happen, but everything eventually fell into place.

Once, when we were playing, the thing grew. It was my fault, obviously, as I had used my magic without Andrew having any part in it. But something else happened and I had no idea what was going on. We had been in my bedroom, and he raced out. The only thing I had heard him say was, 'Oh my God, it's huge.' My immediate thought was that I had hurt him. There can't have been anyone else in the house that time because Andrew was making odd, strange noises, and he would never have risked anyone hearing him. I know now exactly what he was doing, but I was so worried then. I tried to hide under my bedclothes but after a while I thought that I needed to go and see if he was all right. I had heard strange, moaning noises coming from the bathroom, and I could only think he was very unwell, thanks to me.

As I was trying to pluck up courage to go to Andrew, he called my name. 'Lorraine! Come through here for a minute, will you?' he shouted. I followed his voice to the bathroom and when I saw him, he looked as if he was in pain. He was standing, masturbating, but gave me no indication that this was fine, that he was enjoying it. He left me to think it was painful and that I had hurt him.

I didn't know what he was doing with his hand, but he told me not to worry. He comforted me when he was done, and said it was fine. I was certainly led to believe that this was something which was entirely my fault and that I could get in trouble for bringing about. This happened often. He would run off to the bathroom, seemingly in pain, and I would be terrified, thinking he would die, and then he would forgive me. In a bizarre twist, I started to think that he would tell on me. I worried that the police would come to the door and I would be in trouble. The intensity of my fear and the mixed emotions it caused was overwhelming.

Getting him to 'grow' and seeing him masturbating himself went on regularly, but he would also get me to touch him. To begin with, he would suggest that I stroke him to see what would happen. 'See if your magic finger works today.' If it didn't do what he expected, he would tell me to try again until it did grow. Initially, he was clothed when this went on, but, unsurprisingly, one day it fell out. Sometimes we'd be sitting, sometimes we'd be rolling around wrestling, but it was always like a game. It was always as if I was instigating it and he had no part in it, no control over it.

He used my name throughout, especially when he started to groan. I couldn't differentiate between what was good and what was bad. What was good and what was serious. I assumed others did these things because he made out that it was entirely normal.

On the day that it 'fell' out, he said that I should touch it and see what happened, as usual. I don't think I even saw it as part of him. That may sound odd, but it was in a different form to what I had seen. I knew that boys and men urinated from those things, but this looked peculiar. I didn't know if it was part of him or whether it was something he had put in his trousers. We had done no sex education in school, I was far too young, and there was no sex on television in those days, so I hadn't seen anything that may have opened my eyes to sex.

'Don't worry,' he said, 'I won't tell on you.'

Again, I worried that I had done something he would tell others about. Was I hurting him when I used my magic to make this thing so big? I even looked it up in an encyclopaedia once. I checked to see what that part of bodies looked like and whether you could kill someone by making it grow. I had that fear for such a long time. I was terrified that I would do it to someone else. What if I hurt someone just when I walked past them or sat beside them at school? If I had this magic inside me, it could happen anywhere and everywhere, couldn't it?

That first time, I was petrified. If I touched it with my hand when there were no clothes on it, perhaps something even worse would occur. I couldn't bring myself to touch him. He looked cross but a forced smile soon came on his face and he said he would help me to get the magic out.

'Give me your hand,' he said, reaching out to me. 'Let's see what you can do today.' It worked. The magic worked. Once it grew, Andrew went to the toilet and I heard the

75

usual groans. That was very confusing. He had asked me to use the magic and he must have known what could happen – why would he do that if it was going to hurt him?

I soon learned to do it anyway. It was what he expected. In the early days, he always went to the bathroom to masturbate himself to ejaculation. He was a fastidious man. I can't imagine he would risk messing his trousers. When I was older, I would do that for him, but that was later. Sometimes, when he was in the bathroom, he would call me through to watch him. It was very rare that I refused. When I did, it was because I was still scared of what I had done, but he knew just how to punish me for my refusal. He simply withdrew his affection. At that stage, that was the worst thing imaginable for me.

Andrew always told me what was nice. I didn't get to choose. When we did these things (by 'we', I mean that I was physically there, but there was certainly no informed consent – I was a child), he would tell me that it was lovely, that it felt good, that I liked it. It was the most horrendous abuse of trust, for let's not forget what he was saying I liked, what he was saying was lovely. A grown man, the only person who had ever shown me love, the only person I trusted, was making me touch his genitals and telling me I liked it. He was inserting his fingers into me and saying it was lovely. He was using me for his sexual pleasure and saying that it was all down to me, it was my magic, and that I adored every second of it.

I believed it all. I believed I had caused it all and I had

made him do these things. His lack of control was put at my door and it was all falsely presented to me as my enticement of him. He was unable to hold himself back because of me. It was the same message I had heard all of my life – everything was my fault, as always. It was my fault Mum hated me. It was my fault Andrew abused me. Everything was down to me.

CHAPTER 7

FIONA

Someday I'll find a gun
And you will run, not me.

The other main thing in my life at this age was starting school. Mum had never attempted to send me to nursery again, not after the shame of the first and last time – but she couldn't stop school. I loved it from the moment I started. It was a safe place, a place where I could be invisible and feel secure because I wouldn't be hit. It was certainly an easier place to be in those first years than home.

Another wonderful revelation for me was that I was clever. The teachers liked this, so I could avoid their wrath, but I also had to be careful to blend in, not to stand out. I was afraid to be seen. I watched adults. I always watched adults. I needed to know what they were doing and, because of this, I was quiet and studious. I didn't really care what the children were up to – they had no power. I think that came from my mum's behaviour. I never knew when she would turn, so I thought if I watched adult behaviour closely enough I would be able to predict it.

Locking myself in a bubble to observe and not be observed didn't last, however, because I soon became aware and horrified by the amount of bullying I saw all around me. The teachers seemed to do very little about it. I was so badly treated by my mum at home that I found it very hard to bear seeing such behaviour at school, too.

I still found it hard to make friends. I probably didn't try, to be honest. I didn't have the capacity to play or inter-act like a normal child, so when I was forced into a non-learning environment, such as playtime, I was lost again. On top of this, I was still neglected, still hungry, and still something of an odd child. The other children soon learned to stay away from me, as I didn't know how to engage with them. I was never really bullied myself because I never reacted. If other kids called me names, I wouldn't do anything, I'd just stand there. They didn't matter to me, they were insignificant. Even on the occasions when some-one hit me, I did nothing.

There was only one other girl who I could imagine being a friend at all. Her name was Fiona and the reason we could potentially get on was that we were both oddballs. I didn't speak to her, and I certainly didn't play with her, but we both stood at opposite ends of the playground, completely alone and completely disengaged. I felt like we had a bond, but I wasn't overly keen to take it any further.

She looked as if she had been dragged through a hedge backwards. She never looked washed or clean, and there was a stench that came from her and filled the classroom. It didn't really bother me. I knew why I looked and acted the way I did and, even at that young age, I suspected Fiona must have similar reasons.

I had no idea, though, that the reasons were even more similar than I could ever have imagined. Fiona was my first friend but the circumstances of that friendship were odd. From standing alone at opposite ends of the playground, we gradually ended up side by side, not communicating at first, but standing together nonetheless.

When we did eventually start talking to each other, it was stilted. We had that kind of friendship where you didn't have to say anything, you almost thought the same things at the same time; we didn't need to talk. Neither of us had the skills to develop a real conversation or friendship, but we did what we could. The other kids largely left us alone, as we were the oddballs, and we never ran about happily like they did.

She wasn't too bright and she was a nervous wee character but one day Fiona surprised me a lot.

'D'you want to come to my house?' she asked.

I had never been invited to another child's house before. I didn't know what would be expected of me, but I liked the idea of being away from home.

I nodded.

'I'll ask,' I said.

There was no resistance from my mum. 'About time,' she said. 'Thought you'd never get a pal.'

I went to Fiona's house after school, a few things in my

bag for the sleepover. To be honest, it never struck me that there would be any danger in the situation because, for me, all of the danger in my life was associated with things from home. Although Fiona was odd like me, I didn't think about why that was the case. I should have known.

She came from a big family. Although we were poor, they had even less, and I don't think any of them worked. I had never felt any sense of superiority before, but when I went to Fiona's house I remember thinking that it wasn't very nice and it smelled and it wasn't clean. My house was always clean. As a child, you take a sense of superiority where you find it. There was nothing nice in that house whatsoever. Ours wasn't like that – Mum had her reputation to think of, and she would never have allowed the sort of squalor I saw in Fiona's house. There were very few rooms and everyone seemed to congregate in the living room. There was a sofa there which pulled out into a bed and Fiona said that's where we would be sleeping later. This seemed like a great novelty to me, as I had never seen such a thing, and I looked forward to bedtime.

There were no rules, people were coming and going constantly. You could go into the kitchen and make a sandwich whenever you liked, which had never happened to me before. Her parents didn't seem to be in charge. I found that difficult, as I wasn't used to other people apart from in a classroom where there was at least some order. I wasn't used to chaos.

When it got dark, her parents unfolded the sofa and I climbed in with my little friend. It seemed like great fun –

but it didn't last. There were no lights in the room, perhaps their electricity had been cut off or they couldn't afford the meter, but the darkness was only vaguely lit by street lamps. Fiona and I settled under the covers – a few tatty threadbare blankets and a pile of smelly coats – and giggled. I thought that we'd just be left there to fall asleep; I had no idea that this family had their own perversions.

Almost as soon as Fiona and I got into bed, there were other bodies there, too. It was clearly how they lived. This whole family just existed on top of one another and there didn't seem to be any control coming from anyone. Again, I felt a little bit superior that in my family there wasn't this sort of behaviour. My Uncle Andrew was kind (apart from some mishaps which I caused), but this was not nice. It actually felt incredibly scary and out of control because I had no idea who was in the bed with us. What was clear was, regardless of age, they all thought it was fine to touch one another.

There was no way of getting out. There were no mobile phones in those days and, anyway, I knew my mum would have gone mad if I'd tried to get away. It would have shown her up, I guess. I just had to endure it.

Over the course of that night, the father and her four brothers (all older than us, all teenagers), were in and out of that bed constantly. It was horrible, but what struck me most was that Fiona seemed to accept it. It appeared to be normal to her. It also seemed to me that it was why she was how I was; why we were the same. They were all mastur-bating and touching each other, and I had no idea who was where, where one person began and another ended. They were all there at the same time, lots of bodies in a bed, all touching each other.

They began to abuse me. They didn't go as far as Andrew had gone – part of that might have been because I did show some resistance. The touching and the hands and bodies worried me. I didn't like touching and I wasn't used to it. One of the boys was quite rough and again I wasn't used to that. They were touching me intimately and they were pushing against me. They were trying to force me to have sex and I was resisting that. They were seeing how far they could go, without a doubt.

What I realised was that Fiona – who was lying next to me – was crying at everything. She was really distressed, sobbing quietly every time she was touched. It seemed that this was the normal way her family worked. I've thought back to that night and they behaved as if it was all so normal; that just must have been her life for her. I remember at one point trying to push someone away who was trying to touch me. I heard him tut as if he was just frustrated that he wouldn't get to do what he wanted. He wasn't angry, just annoyed and a bit confused that someone was resisting him, I think. These were people I didn't know so I had a sense to some degree that this was my body and it was wrong; it wasn't Andrew.

It was freaky but it was also strange because it established that what was happening with Andrew really was normal. It didn't seem right, something inside me knew that, but I was getting messages from another source that it was normal. It happens, people keep quiet about it, but it's everywhere. I had thought I was an alien, that there was something wrong with me. But that night, I found out that it happened in lots of families. I thought it was just a horrible world that I lived in. In fact, that night at Fiona's house reinforced for me that this was what happened in families. I knew that now.

I never went back. I didn't need to. There was nothing good for me there – all I had learned was that it happened. It happened everywhere. I was six years old.

CHAPTER 8

FRIENDS

One day all kids will be free,
And safe and happy ... maybe.

New Year was always a time for parties. It was a great
excuse for adults to get as drunk as possible, and I remember that there would be singing, dancing, and alcohol
flowing for days on end. We would all go to other people's
houses, too, and it seemed as if that whole period after
Christmas was just one big drunken festival.

Of course, when Andrew was at home, there was always
a party atmosphere, but New Year made it happen in everyone's house. I recall being about six when one such
gathering was taking place in our living room. Mum was in
a good mood as she was the centre of attention. There were
lots of people around, all of whom had brought even more
drink, and a few of them were starting to dance in the
middle of the room. There was the occasional vague
drunken warbling going on, too. The atmosphere was
good-natured. Lots of children were in there, and I just

watched, not really interacting with anyone and also hoping that no one would notice me.

I wished Andrew would arrive and, after a few hours, my wishes came true. When the door opened and I saw him, I could feel a change in the room. He wasn't alone that night, as he had brought a friend with him who I heard other people refer to as Derek.

Within minutes of his arrival, Andrew had sought me out. He came over to the corner where I was sitting (or hiding), and crouched down on the floor beside me. 'Hello there,' he said. 'How's my favourite girl?'

I smiled and hugged him back as he put his arms around me. 'You being a good girl?' he asked. I nodded. 'Of course you are, of course you are. Now, you just sit there and I'll see you later, all right?' I could hear people shouting his name, they all wanted Andrew to come and see them, talk to them, sing for them, but he had chosen to speak to me before anyone else. 'I'll be back,' he said, pressing a chocolate bar into my hand and walking off.

He disappeared into a group of people. It was as if his presence had taken the party to a different level, and the noise and laughter increased. I knew he would come back to me at some point, I knew he wouldn't forget me. I sat there, clutching my bar of chocolate and feeling so special that he had noticed me. I waited a while. The room was getting hotter and hotter, and the noise was becoming louder and louder. Every so often, as I looked over to Uncle Andrew, I would catch his eye. He'd smile or wink, and I'd feel secure, warm in the knowledge that he loved me. His friend Derek stayed by his side throughout the evening. At one point, Andrew came over to me with a pint in his hand. 'Here you go,' he said, 'you must be thirsty under there.' He passed me the glass and I drained the dregs from it. 'Good girl,' he said, as always.

When he walked away, a woman laughed. 'Setting her on the wrong path, Andrew?' she said, merrily. She walked over to me with a smaller glass. 'There you are,' she giggled, 'have that!' I don't know what it was, perhaps sherry, but Andrew nodded in encouragement, and I drained that one, too.

It started a trend. I could even see my mother smiling a little as people brought drinks over regularly for the rest of the night, passing the last bits of their booze to me in the corner, then walking away in laughter when I handed back the empty glasses. Throughout it all, Andrew smiled indulgently, so I kept going.

Eventually I couldn't fight the tiredness which had been trying to claim me. It was getting late and the heat of the room made it impossible for me to keep my eyes open. I was also, very probably, drunk. I remember feeling very dozy underneath the table, but I don't recall anyone picking me up. However, they must have done, for the next thing I knew I was in my bed.

I had woken up – not because of the noise of the party, which was still going on, but because someone was touching me. It was dark and I was still half asleep – and half drunk – but I knew there was someone there. My head hurt and I was really thirsty. It was also really cold. I knew that there had been lots of coats on my bed earlier in the evening, as there always was at parties, but I was now shivering. There were no blankets on me, no coats, and I was only wearing a vest.

I was trying to process all of this as well as coming to terms with the fact that there was a man stroking my body. His hands were all over me, and he was breathing heavily, as if he had been running.

'What are you doing?' I asked.

'Ssh,' he whispered. 'Be quiet. There's a good girl.'

I knew him. He was the man who had come to the party with Andrew. The man I'd heard the others call Derek.

'Now, you have to be quiet,' he went on. 'If you're not quiet, your Uncle Andrew will be angry with you, won't he?'

At the time, all I could think was that I didn't want that. When I think back to it as an adult, I realise that it was very early proof of how Andrew had been grooming me and setting me up for his friends to abuse.

'Come here,' Derek said, shifting up the bed to be closer to me. 'You're shivering. I'll warm you up.' I didn't want him to 'warm me up', I didn't want him to touch me or to be there at all but, more than anything, I didn't want Andrew to be angry with me. Derek picked me up and put me on his lap. 'Do you want to play?' he asked. I shook my head. 'Andrew says you like to play. Do you want to play horsey?' Again, I was confused. I definitely did not want to play horsey with him, but I wanted to please Andrew.

I could hear the party still going on with people coming

and going. I was on Derek's lap, and he was touching me again. There was no pretence at playing; he was just doing whatever he wanted. Although I wasn't being physically hurt, everything felt wrong. It was as if things were completely disjointed. I was in the wrong world. I was listening to everyone having fun, except me.

As I was sitting there on his lap, wondering why he was doing these things, someone knocked on my bedroom door. That was very unusual. In fact, I don't think it had ever happened before. There was no real privacy in our house, and there was certainly none shown towards children in those days. The knock was quick and sharp and, as soon as it sounded, Derek jumped up from my bed and left the room. It must have been a sign. It had to be. Perhaps he was being warned that someone was coming, or he had been missed; whatever it was, he knew to leave.

What happened that night set the tone for what would happen at many parties in the years to come. It was as if Andrew had broken me in, made me amenable to these types of men, and what they wanted to do to me. If Andrew was visiting or staying over or babysitting or partying, there was a very high chance that there would be another man – or men – there, too, and that they would abuse me.

That New Year was one I remember well for another reason. Not only was there the party at our house at which I was plied with drink and Derek touched me, but Andrew took me to another party elsewhere. In those days – perhaps it still happens, I don't know – people in Scotland celebrated New Year for a number of days and always with a lot of drink. They would carry a bottle between houses, and everyone would be expected to share and be friendly. There was an atmosphere of jollity and drunkenness for days on end.

One night, just after dinner, Andrew told me that we were going to a party. It would be just the two of us, which thrilled me, but I didn't like the thought that there would be others when we got there. I don't know where the party was but it must have been nearby as we walked. Not that many people had cars, anyway, but I don't recall it being terribly far away.

Andrew held my hand the whole way there and I was glad to be with him, but wary of what was going to happen. The thing which sticks in my mind very clearly was that I was wearing a new dress. Someone had given it to me for Christmas. It was frilly, dark blue with flowers and ribbons. I hated it. I hated all dresses and I preferred to wear trousers so that I didn't stand out. I never thought I was pretty because my mum always told me that I wasn't, and it seemed to me that dresses were for pretty girls, so I always wanted to avoid them. However, I had to wear it because it was a present and because, as I was going out with Andrew, Mum wanted me to look nice. Andrew constantly told me I looked pretty in it. I wanted to believe him, but I had trouble accepting any compliments as I was so unused to them.

The dress felt odd on me, but I had no choice. When we got to the party, it was busy and a few people – men and women – came up to me and said I looked nice. They were friendly enough; they asked me what I'd got for Christmas and whether I was having a good time out for the night with my kind Uncle Andrew. I said as little as possible, and stuck by his side.

I recognised some of the people there. They weren't family, but there were 'aunties' and 'uncles'. Everyone was drinking a lot, as usual, and I was given some, too, as soon as I got there. I think it was probably sherry. Everyone smiled at me and they were all perfectly pleasant. I felt special and quite grown up to be included in all of this. Andrew was very attentive. He stayed beside me even when everyone was demanding his attention, and I let my guard down. I felt safe.

Then I saw Derek.

That threw me a little. I'd hated what had happened a few days earlier, and the memory of waking up in my bed, almost naked with him touching me, chilled me to the bone. He seemed to be looking over at me every time I stole a glance his way, so I gripped Andrew's hand a little tighter, breathing a sigh of relief every time he squeezed back. I still hadn't made the link – I still didn't realise that Andrew was the common denominator.

After a while, one of the men crouched down beside me so that he was at my height. Andrew was talking to some other people as this man commented on my dress.

'Don't you look pretty tonight?' he said. 'I bet everyone always says what a lovely little thing you are, don't they?'

I didn't know how to respond. People most certainly did

not always say what a lovely little thing I was, and it was completely alien to me even to think that someone who said such a thing might be telling the truth. The man twirled the hem of my dress and again said that I was very pretty. He took my hand and said to Andrew that he wanted to show me something. My uncle smiled and said that was fine. His only parting words to me, as the man led me away, were, 'Be a good girl.'

I was taken to a bedroom. 'You look so pretty in that dress that I'd really like to take a picture of you,' he said. 'Is that OK?' I nodded. His request seemed innocent enough. 'Good. Good. I've got a friend here who's really good at taking photos, so he'll make sure it's lovely. Won't that be nice?'

I nodded again. I hadn't noticed the man standing against the wall but, as I watched him now, I could see that he was taking things out of a bag. He had a large, very professional-looking camera with him.

I wasn't used to pictures being taken of me. When I was young, most people didn't have a camera, and many people still went to photographers' studios once a year to get a family portrait done. I was shy and self-aware, but the man who had taken me into the room kept saying I was lovely, that I was a very pretty little girl, and that I should always be photographed so that everyone could see how gorgeous I was.

As he spoke, the other man snapped away.

I don't think it would take a genius to work out what happened next. As time went on, the man took my clothes off and made sure that I was photographed with him, in various states of undress and naked. Andrew wasn't in the room at any point, but other men were. There was a steady procession of them. When the first man had got all of the staged pictures he wanted, he left and another one came in. This happened about six times. Each time a different man, each time their own sordid fantasies acted out for photographs.

They were very careful to make sure that one man left before another came in. In fact, they were all always very careful about anything which could lead to corroboration. They all acted out their own requests. One man put me over his knee and pretended to smack me. There was no actual physical abuse and I can only think that was one of the rules for that scenario. I assume that these men had been told they could have me for that night, they could take photos, but they couldn't hit me. There was definitely some sort of barrier because none of them hurt me despite them obviously having very unnatural desires regarding small children. I was touched sexually, but nothing was forced into me and I wasn't slapped or punched at any point. It was all a bit of a blur. I seemed to be constantly on someone's lap. One man had no sooner left the room than another would come in.

When they had all got what they wanted, I was told to get dressed and then taken back through to the room where the party was taking place. Andrew was there, still talking to people, and he smiled at me. I was given some food and something to drink, and the party went on. It was all so normal – the abuse itself was completely normalised. I don't remember going home at the end of the night, but I do know that nothing was said to me about the whole situation by Andrew. He never did refer to anything like that in advance or once it had happened, and neither did I. I had already worked out the rules.

CHAPTER 9

MY STRANGE WORLD

He loves me so he hurts me
To try and make me good.
It doesn't work. I'm just too bad
And don't do what I should.

My memory has so many different sections and, like all survivors, there are so many compartments with so many triggers. I'll remember a smell which reminds me of a man which reminds me of a place which reminds me of another man who I think was with a woman who had a certain smell – and I'm back to square one. This is the case for most survivors, I believe. When we try to put together our pasts, the triggers are many and varied, the memories are disjointed – and why wouldn't they be? We were children. Even someone with an idyllic childhood who is only trying to remember the lovely things which happened to them will scratch their head and wonder who gave them that doll and was it for Christmas or their third birthday? Did they have a party when they were four or five? When did they go on a plane for the first time? You see, even happy memories are hard to piece together – so imagine how hard it is to collate all of the trauma, to pull together all of the things I've been trying to push away for so many years.

My world was getting stranger and more complicated by the day. The only love I got was from someone who abused me. The only time I got compliments was in situations where I was being primed to be abused again. I could barely work out what was real and what was normal. I had two lives and I didn't want either of them. Andrew's friends were now part of the horror of my secret world and I had no way of getting out of it. All I knew was that no one would believe the horrible, nasty little girl if she spoke out. The only person I trusted was my Uncle Andrew. I had no one else. And it was about to get even worse.

Mum was becoming more and more frustrated with me. Where we lived was rough and there were always fights between children, usually over nothing. She used to despair about my refusal to hit back. I hated violence and she thrived on it. I know that she used to watch from the window of our house because sometimes she would shout down to me when there was a scuffle. 'Lorraine! Don't just stand there! Get stuck in!'

The fights were never important and the last thing I wanted was to 'get stuck in'. One day, another girl had taken a dislike to me for something, I can't even remember what, and she was trying to goad me into a fight. She was pushing me and shoving me, and the other kids were standing round trying to get a scrap going. I was completely disengaged and did nothing. Without any warning, Mum appeared. 'Are you just going to stand there and let her get away with that?' she screamed at me. Yes. Yes, I was, but I couldn't tell her that. 'Come on! Fight back!' she yelled. I didn't want to fight. There was nothing I wanted to fight about, nothing was that important, it was just little kids filling their time in the middle of desperate, dreary lives.

In a flash, my mum grabbed my hand and held it up, swinging it at the other girl and forcing me, through her actions, to slap her. I was horrified. Technically, I had hit this girl, even though I had done nothing but stand there. Mum did it a few times more before she was satisfied, then she stomped off home, leaving me there, ashamed. I had seen her do this – forcing someone to hit someone else – before but that time it had been aimed at me. I had annoyed her in some way and she had spent the whole day stomping about saying that when my dad got home, I'd be 'for it'. As soon as he got in the door, she launched herself on him, saying how bad I'd been and how much I deserved a leathering. Dad looked exhausted as he slumped down in his chair. This wasn't good enough for Mum. She stormed off to their bedroom, came back with a leather belt, and wrapped it round his hand. 'Belt her!' she shrieked. 'Belt her!'

She lifted his hand up and practically forced him to do it. There was no enthusiasm in that beating from my dad; he was clearly doing it to shut his wife up. It should have been a warning to me of her methods. I was sickened that she had used the same thing on me because, from as far back as

I could recall, I couldn't bear violence. Even though it happened to me all the time, I genuinely felt that no one should be hit. It was just wrong. It was a huge, absolute truth inside of me, and it would be challenged horribly.

Andrew moved to a house in the same street as us at some point when I was around five or six. There were still a lot of parties, even though he lived nearby.

The abuse was getting more invasive as time went on. I would only really notice it when he hurt me, but I was even getting used to that. Obviously, he was ramping up the severity – and it was only a matter of time before he would rape me. He was preparing me for that by constantly touching and invading me. I have absolutely no wish or inclination to go into the detail of that, and I can't see why anyone would want me to, but I am sure that it is quite obvious to anyone reading this how he prepared me. Given that he had been touching and 'interfering' with me for so long, my body was used to these assaults. Anyone who plans to abuse a child fully knows that the body of that child will be unused to adult invasion, and the clever ones set up those children so that the full scale of the invasion will be as seamless as possible. He increased what he did, and my body was given warning of what was going to happen, even if I didn't realise it.

He was always ready to play with me. As a child who didn't play well, and who craved play at the same time, it was all I had. I would laugh; that was a rare thing for me. But I also remember it being coupled with unease. I was always trying to please him. I wanted to do things that would please him. I would dance about, I would attempt to sing. I would desperately try to engage him. If he was talking to my parents, I would try to get his attention, even though I was so shy. I would slide over and sit on his lap. At one point, he said to me, 'You're a real wee tease, aren't you?' I didn't even know what he meant. He would say, 'You've taken a real shine to me, haven't you? You'd do anything for your Uncle Andrew.'

He would tickle me and wrestle with me on the floor. In the beginning, he initiated the physical contact, now he put it onto me. He'd say, 'You never leave me alone, do you? What a demanding wee girl you are. I don't think you'd give me a second's peace, given half a chance.' As time went on, I knew what he liked, so I would be demonstrative and initiate play. That was an important shift. He managed to turn it round so that what I was doing was seeing him and clicking into a personality which wasn't me. I was the Lorraine he wanted. I was what he expected.

This was psychological grooming alongside sexual grooming. I wasn't just allowing him to do what he wanted to my body, I was changing my personality for him. Andrew made me into a child who was well-prepared to accept the advances of men. The foundations were laid by him. I knew not to tell about these things. I knew not to talk. I knew that you smiled even when it didn't come naturally. I knew to be whatever someone else wanted me to be. I would have walked on fire for him. I would have gone to the moon and back. I would have given him everything – and I did.

He was my only hope. I had given up ever thinking that anyone else would love me. The only thing I had in my life apart from Uncle Andrew were books. I'd read anything and everything. Magazines, adverts, graffiti. Anything. I particularly loved books about animals because I adored them. We didn't have any pets at this stage because my mum wouldn't allow it, but I looked out for them everywhere. Whenever I was on the streets, I'd be searching for strays. You knew where you were with animals. I loved wildlife and nature, the innocence of it all drew me in. I was the sort of child who wanted to know every detail about whatever I was interested in. I loved the library and got books which would tell me every breed of dog, every type of tree, every species of insect.

It was all safe. When I got into stories, I could disappear. The thing I got into trouble with at school was reading too much, if that was possible. I steeped myself in it. Facts were my big love. Fiction was harder. When I tried to read Enid Blyton, it just seemed too unreal. All of the children had ridiculous names and everyone liked each other. They were all nice people and there was nothing for me to relate to. I knew that if you scratched the veneer of what seemed respectable and good, there would be something very different underneath, so fiction meant nothing to me. I would look at people and wonder what they were really like, and this feeling that everyone had a facade was something I was finding more and more evidence of.

Nothing felt real. I didn't even feel real to myself. In school, I managed to be top of the class a few times, so I

made a point of moving away from that so I remained unno-
ticed. I had to get learning elsewhere. I had to sneak books
into the house as they weren't 'approved of' by Mum. To
my shame, the only thing I ever stole in my life was a
book – it was *Call of the Wild* by Jack London. We'd started
reading the story in class and I couldn't bear the wait. I
trotted off to the library but I couldn't get it out, so I went
to a bookshop, found it, and put it up my jumper. I intended
to put it back, even though that was a ridiculous idea as it
would have been used, but I never did. I just had to keep it.
I needed it.

I also started to write. We had a vegetable plot outside
the house, as lots of people did in those days. I was responsible for it because, to all intents and purposes, I was the
eldest child. Within the vegetable plot, underneath my
potatoes, I had a box. In there was everything, all my scraps
of paper, all my scribbling, my stories and my poems. When
I lifted potatoes up or put some in, I'd add bits of paper, too.
I'd clear it out periodically. The box didn't last very well. I
moved on to bits of cloth wrapped up in each other and put
in a tin. They were all very precious to me and I lived in
terror of the tin being found. So many others things were
found, there was so very little that I had been able to keep
private, whether it was a book I was reading that someone
could exploit or a feeling that Andrew seemed to know I
had. It seemed as if someone was always watching me.

A couple of times I had also written poems and stories in
the classroom which showed, partly, how I was feeling. I
attempted to do this through my artwork, too. It didn't go

down well, to say the least. My parents were informed that I was doing 'odd' things, that there was something wrong with me because I was doing dark and sinister work. I don't think I was explicitly trying to tell anyone anything; it was just spilling out. I couldn't keep it in, what was going on, what was being done to me.

Reading and my love for animals gave me a way to survive. I would need everything I could get.

CHAPTER 10

HURT

Children don't know what to do
When adults tell us lies.
We wait for God to help
But he does not hear our cries.

A lot of paedophiles work by identifying the 'right' type of child. They're very good at reading people and developing the psychology. That is just what Andrew did. He built on the little girl who was there and made her what he wanted and needed her to be. I was a blank canvas. I was ready to be prepared for even more appalling acts by others.

I don't think I even had the language to tell. I didn't have any concept of what was happening or the wrongness of it. Until I was about eight, all I thought about was keeping the one loving person in my life. Once he raped me, though, it changed.

It was Easter when it finally happened. I'm sure he had been building up to it; he had certainly been trying to prepare me physically for what he was about to do. There was a party in our house, and I knew that Andrew was planning to stay over, as he often did. Even though he had his own house and it was nearby, he slept at ours whenever something was going on, or when he babysat.

That night, everyone was very drunk. There was great hilarity and I had been watching it all, as usual. As the night wore on, I was getting very sleepy. No one had tried to give me drink that evening, but it was hot and noisy. I was sent to bed by Mum, and I was glad to go.

At some point, I was woken up by Andrew coming into my bed. He had done that before, though, so it didn't seem unusual. It was common for him to be told to go and sleep in my room. That may beggar belief for many people reading this, and I'm not surprised. To tell an adult man to go and sleep in a little girl's bed takes an awful lot of trust or an awful lot of stupidity on the part of the parents. There were a limited number of beds, but to tell someone to climb in with the bairn seems a shocking solution. In most families, perhaps the child would be taken into the parents' room, if another person needed to sleep over, but that wasn't the sort of family I had.

It was abnormal and so wrong, but that's not how I saw it. I was completely innocent.

When I woke up, he was already raping me. He wasn't trying; he was actually raping me. I remember the shock of the physical pain more than anything. I didn't know what was going on. I had no idea what this was. I couldn't conceptualise it. I couldn't have put it into words.

As a child, I knew he had a penis because he had made me

touch it and I had seen it grow hard. I knew that when I sat on his lap, I could feel it, but it had never occurred to me that this man could invade me. I didn't actually know what he was doing. I didn't know what he was putting in there.

It was alien to me.

I think he made a mistake. I think he was so well on course to grooming me that he hadn't planned for it to happen like that, but he was drunk and took his opportunity. That was the point when I began to change.

'Look what you've made me do.' He was clearly annoyed with me.

He was saying the same things he had always said. It was my fault. I had done this. I had made him lose control. Just by being there; just by being a child. By saying it was my fault he absolved himself of all responsibility. He had come into my room, he had lain in my bed, he had shoved my nightie up, he had taken his clothes off, he had pushed himself into me, he had raped me. A child. But, according to him, it was the child's fault, not his.

When he raped me, it was agony. The scariest thing was that I bled. I knew that wasn't normal. When he fell asleep, I managed to squeeze out of bed and go to the bathroom. I wiped myself and realised that there was blood there. I was frightened and couldn't really work out what had happened. Why was I bleeding? You bled from cuts, so I thought that was why I was bleeding. I was too young to know about periods, so I had simply never thought or known that blood could come from there.

Then, a horrible thought occurred to me – maybe the

blood wasn't mine! What if it was Andrew's? What if I had hurt him rather than the other way around?

I tried to wash the blood off me but the hardest thing was trying not to cry. It was the biggest struggle I'd had in a long time, but I was determined not to give in. I'd made that decision a while ago but my head was bursting. I had no concept of how to fix this.

The bathroom was dark – I wasn't allowed to put lights on at night – but there was enough brightness coming in from street lamps for me to see the blood. And, of course, I could feel it. I was so sore. I was burning and aching, I was wet and sticky. I tried to wash myself, not knowing what to do for the best. I was biting down hard on my lip the whole time as I could feel the tears starting. I had to hurt myself even more to stop it. I didn't want to cry or make a noise, and I couldn't risk anyone knowing. They were all drunk by now and in bed, but I still feared that someone could hear.

I kept thinking back to how annoyed Andrew had seemed. What if he told on me? It was my fault; he'd said so. What if this was the final straw for him? In reality, he had got drunk and moved on too quickly with his grooming process. It was an indication of how deeply I was controlled by him, that I didn't think screaming was an option. Surely, if I had, and someone had seen a child with blood and semen all over her, surely they would have done something?

I thought if I made a noise the police would come and get me. That was how twisted everything was in my mind.

How would I know otherwise?

There will be people who simply can't imagine what this whole building-up process was like. They just won't understand why I didn't tell. I can only explain it in the same way that domestic violence works. If a person has no experience of, or sympathy with, that situation, they will look at someone who is being hurt or battered every day by a man, and they will judge the woman. They say, 'That would never happen to me.' What they don't realise is that, when she first met him, he was really nice. He bought her flowers, paid attention to her, they fell in love. It was all perfectly normal. It is only over a long period of time that she became eroded of self-confidence and self-esteem in a way that could happen to anybody at all. That is the key – it could happen to anybody at all. Whether it is him controlling the money very slowly and making excuses for it, moving on to a slap and making excuses for it, people begin to accommodate things.

If we take this back to a child who knows absolutely nothing, who has grown up without love and is searching for it, they grasp love when it appears. Whether they like it or loathe it, they grab it. Everyone needs love, I think. You grab it so hard because you can't risk losing the chance.

And when you love someone as a child – and as an adult – you accept mistakes, you accept when things aren't quite right. You accommodate. If you are then blamed for the things which happen, it makes it even more difficult for the person at the heart of it to realise what is going on. It's too easy for those on the outside to say they would have done something differently. They will say, 'Why didn't you just tell?' But how would I have done that? Who would I have told? And what about the fear of what would happen? If you believe you have done something wrong because you have been made to believe you have done something wrong, then you are the guilty party.

That's what I was. I was the guilty party, not Andrew. If anyone had said anything against him, I'd have been quick to defend him. That probably lasted beyond childhood, actually, into adulthood. The dynamic which is set up between abuser and abused is a very strong one – he needs you to stay quiet and do these things and comply; you need him to give you some affection and love. Eventually, the abuse doesn't seem as bad. Sometimes, the lack of love is the real problem. For all of the people who have had it, whose parents hugged them when they were little, this will be a horrible idea. They have never been denied it, so they don't know. They don't know how they would respond.

I have thought about this a lot. When I was older, I did blame myself. I thought I was stupid not to tell, but experience has shown me there are lots of different aspects to every story.

I didn't tell, but I also have no doubts I would never, ever have been believed. There would have had to be a trusting adult or a trusting friend before a child like me could have told. Even hindsight tells me there was no one there for me, no one available for me to disclose to. As a child, I think you do what you do instinctively. You just get on. Unless you have been taught that it is OK to talk, it is

OK to tell – the things we should be teaching children – you don't see it as an option. If a child is never told, 'Those are your private parts, this is your body, and no one should ever touch you,' how can they know? I was never told any of that. It would have been a simple thing to tell me, it's a simple thing to tell any child.

I didn't know what sex was – and yet I had been raped. I didn't know those words. All I knew was that I was hurt and I was so ashamed. I felt disgusting, I felt dirty. I felt I was the most shameful thing on the planet. Where could I go with that? That sense of horror and shame is still with me. I lost my faith that night. The first glimmer of doubt regarding God came into my mind that evening, and my faith would never come back.

When I went back to bed from the bathroom, having cleaned myself up as best I could in the dark and in silence, Andrew was still there. He was fast asleep and stinking of booze. I crawled in through the bottom of the bed and lay awake for hours. I pretended to be asleep when it got light and Andrew got up to leave. I was still in shock. The world had turned over for me, the colours were different. Actually, everything was different.

I went into school and I didn't know up from down. I had been altered. Everything had been altered. I went through the motions that day and when school ended, I lay on my bed until night came. At bedtime, I got down on my knees and prayed, but it meant nothing. The Lord's Prayer just seemed like empty words.

I remembered stories from Sunday school.

Jesus was supposed to love me, He loved all children. God was supposed to love me. I reasoned that, if He knew what was happening, He'd stop it. Maybe the only reason God hadn't stopped it, was that He was too busy, He hadn't been watching so He didn't know what was going on.

I let this brew in my head for a while. I needed to pray, I knew that, but I didn't do it immediately because I wanted to revel in the hope that I had found. One night, when I knew Andrew was back from leave again, I got down on my knees at the side of my bed. I put my all into it; everything I had went into that prayer. With my hands together, I begged him: please God, if there is a God, please come and help me. Take me away, please. Help me, please help me. I said it over and over again, all through the night. I was cold and exhausted, but I was desperate for this God, this Jesus, so I prayed for hours.

I got more specific as the prayers went on, even if I didn't have the exact words. Please don't let 'that' happen again. Please don't let him do 'that' to me. I was asking for the rape to stop, but I didn't know what to call it.

While I was praying, I heard the doorbell and I heard Andrew come in. I jumped into bed and closed my eyes. I lay there for hours, listening to them all laughing and drinking, not knowing whether God had heard me. I didn't know whether I wanted Andrew to leave or not. If he was going to be nice Andrew, then I wanted him here; if he was going to do that thing, I wanted him to disappear. However, surely God had heard me? Surely the thing wouldn't happen again?

That night, he raped me for the second time.

That told me it wasn't true, there was no God. That was the night it dawned on me that there was no hope. Everything was shattered that night and the cracks would just get deeper and deeper. If I had been God, I'd have rescued me – I was only a child, I couldn't do anything, I was asking Him, so if He didn't answer me, that meant there was nothing. It was that simple to me.

What should I do now? I knew there was no God, because I had asked Him for help and He had ignored me. And if there was a God, then he was letting this continue. He was allowing Uncle Andrew to abuse me and rape me and set the scene for others to do the same. As I lay there thinking of what had just happened to me, I knew without doubt that there was no hope. If there was a God, He was on the side of anyone but me, otherwise He would have stopped all of this long ago.

CHAPTER 11

THE WHITE HOUSE

I have to get away from here
I have to run away
I have to get away from fear
I can no longer stay

My family was full of church-going types, including Uncle
Andrew. For us, it was Church of Scotland – Protestantism
with little joy or happiness in God, just misery and warn-
ings. But there was more going on in my life, with regards
to religion, than just church and the Sunday school that I
attended. There was a darker side, which was getting pro-
gressively darker.

While Sunday school and the superficial beliefs of my
family (for it was all superficial – my mum couldn't have
been a truly religious woman, given what she was doing to
me) were providing me with a surface understanding of
God, something else was being taught at night-time. What
was happening then was terribly different.

Uncle Andrew talked to me about religion from an early

stage. I remember one phrase he used a lot. He would say to me, 'It's not about the burning bushes and all of that; there are things which are stronger, things which are more powerful.'

Since other people had joined in my abuse, from the age of about seven, he wasn't the only one saying such words. I was being prepared for the next stage.

One day, when I was playing in the street, a white van pulled up alongside me. I didn't pay much attention to it, largely because I tried not to pay much attention to anything. When I did watch things, I did so surreptitiously. I knew the van was there, but I would never stare open-mouthed at it.

It was one of those small vans, the size of a car, with two front seats and the back half of it closed in. After a little while, as I stayed playing with the dirt and the stones, the passenger door opened.

'Lorraine!' someone called quietly. 'Lorraine!'

I looked up slightly, just from underneath my eyelashes, but I didn't say anything.

'Lorraine!' he said again, almost hissing. 'Get in the van!'

I did hesitate – but only a little. I was a child who was used to being told what to do. The next time he instructed me, I got up, walked to the van and slid in behind the passenger seat, which had been pulled forward.

You need to remember that this all took place during a different time. Of course children still get abused, of course there are still networks of paedophiles, and of course they all have their own methods and ways of identifying victims but, in the early- and mid-1960s, children themselves were defined in a different way. Although a lot of the reaction to child abuse in the current climate is little more than window dressing and empty words, people would – hopefully – find it strange to witness a three-year-old playing with dirt in the gutter day after day. All of the things which should have raised alarm bells when I was little may have done so had they happened today, but none more so, surely, than a van stopping in broad daylight and taking a child away. But taking me was not so big a risk. In those days, children were seen and not heard. Adults had their own lives and children were not expected to be part of that. They were kicked out in the morning for school or during the holidays and not expected to 'bother' anyone for the rest of the day. If I disappeared for a few hours, no one would notice or care. Today, children are told about stranger danger – although the danger is less likely to come from strangers than those known to them. Although these particular men in the van may have been strangers to me, I wasn't an opportunistic 'catch' for them. They knew who I was and they knew I was open to this.

There will no doubt be survivors reading this who recognise how it works, and they will know that likeminded people find each other and they gravitate towards vulnerable children. Once my uncle had found in me that vulnerable child, he provided access to me for others as well.

There were a number of things which made me a vulnerable child. Abusers may package things differently but, fundamentally, they're all the same. It doesn't take them long to find a way in, whether it's offering to babysit, or whether it's listening to a mum at the end of her tether and offering to help, or whether it's just giving an unloved child some attention – all of that is simply the packaging. Some of them will try to excuse it by pretending to love the child, but they're all the same, in my opinion. I believe that. So, not only did Andrew have what he wanted, he prepared me for others.

Now was the time to test just how well he had done his job.

The men in the van took me to a white house and, although I had no idea what was happening, I don't remember being particularly scared or concerned. I was just waiting to see what would happen. I was already groomed, I was already desensitised in many ways. I was kept in the back while we drove, but once we got there, I could see a few things. There were other houses around; it was one in a row. I've actually seen it quite recently. It went up for sale and I wondered whether I should go and look, but it was sold before I could decide. A lot of survivors do that, they go back and look at places to remind themselves, to see if they can remember more, or to see if it was real. It was just a normal residential house on a normal residential street. It had a regular entrance, and a regular front door. There was a bus route very close by. I don't think it was lived in back then, or perhaps it was but the rooms I saw were kept empty of everything apart from what was needed.

I was taken into a big room and there were some other children there. I think there were about six or seven of us. It was unfurnished apart from some tables and chairs around the edges. It was just ordinary furniture, run of the mill and mismatched. The children were sitting on the floor in the middle of the room, with other people – men and women – on the chairs around them. The tables were laden with food. There were sweets and crisps, sandwiches and cakes, biscuits and lollipops. Food wasn't in such plentiful supply back then, not just because it wasn't that long after the war, but because we had different habits. There weren't supermarkets everywhere and there was little disposable income. I was still a hungry child and the only time I got treats was when Andrew gave them to me. It looked like a feast from where I was, and I was immediately more open to being there.

When I walked in, someone clapped their hands and said, 'Come on, then – let's start the party!' but there was no party atmosphere. The children stayed where they were until someone specifically told them to go to the tables and help themselves. I can only guess that they had all been there before. There was no joy in them, no sign that this would be an enjoyable party.

However, nothing really happened that day. It was all incredibly bland. We were allowed to eat whatever we wanted and we were encouraged to play games in the circle.

The adults coordinated all of this, but no one touched me, no one tried to make me do anything. For me, it was absolutely fine. I was given food, I stayed there for a couple of hours, then the white van drove me back and deposited me on my street again, where I resumed playing with the dirt as if nothing had happened.

It became a regular occurrence. Of course it was odd. How strange is it that a child just gets into a vehicle with strangers? And not just one child either. How likely is that? The same hooks will still be happening with children who have no real sense of self. If those kids are set up to be pulled in, you can see it all – if there is someone there who is in the Army, who has good organisational skills and connections, it's even better. Maybe the house belonged to someone in the Army who was away at times, I don't know – I don't have the answers to much of what happened in my childhood. It all went on in broad daylight, usually at a weekend, unless it was a school holiday, with no real attempts to hide anything. They had such arrogance, but then again they weren't doing anything – they were just giving kids sweets, at that point.

Andrew had initiated all of this. The people he introduced me to, the other men like him, had the same views. Sometimes, there were women, but mostly it was men. There always seemed to be parties, there always seemed to be people in my bedroom when he was looking after me or visiting. I was never alone if he was there. My body wasn't my own either and this was just the next stage. As a child

I didn't understand any of this, but what I see now is the grooming that went on with my uncle and then with the other people who were involved. Were these other kids who had been at the party already identified to them? I'd say probably yes. How else would they know who to take? They had to be absolutely certain of getting kids into the pattern of behaviour they wanted, and that came from choosing people who had already been groomed.

When I was taken to the white house, I noticed that the others all wore robes. This didn't seem odd to me either, as I just thought that grown-ups could do what they wanted, and if they chose to do this, then what was the problem? They were only robes, after all.

The robes were different colours, many were red or purple, and the children who were there when I first arrived were wearing white. On my second visit, I was given a white robe, too. It was very plain. They had a pile of them and each child was given any old one once things began, irrespective of whether it fitted or not. So, sometimes the taller kids would have ludicrously short ones on, sometimes there were small children like me who were almost drowned by the amount of fabric they were wearing.

Andrew was never there, but something odd did begin at the white house which would characterise all my future years of abuse. They would call other people Andrew. Sometimes other men, sometimes women. They would tell me to say 'hello' to my Uncle Andrew. They would say that Uncle Andrew had got there before me. He was never there;

it was all part of the process of messing with my mind. I still struggle with names; I don't retain them well. It's no wonder. Practically every man who abused me from that stage onwards was introduced as 'Uncle Andrew'.

It was a different world. I had no idea what was going on, but what was I to do? I can't remember the exact age I was when particular things were done to me, so the notion of analysing it all while it was happening is ridiculous, as I was very young. The way I have tried to do it while writing this is by working out where I lived at the time. I know that I lived in certain houses at certain ages, so, if I remember being taken from one house or another that means that I was a particular age. It's also really important to bear in mind that I was being groomed for some time – Andrew groomed me for others, but there were also events and situations which laid the groundwork for what would come months or even years later.

Nothing illegal or abusive happened at the white house for a while. It was weird and it was spooky but, had I said anything to anyone – the police, any adult who could have been trusted – there was nothing that would have sounded alarming. Yes, I was being taken into a car by strangers who then fed me and made me play games, but that, in itself, would seem odd. I was going into the car voluntarily. There's nothing wrong with feeding a child or asking that child to play, is there? It would all, I'm sure, have sounded like a figment of my imagination. Think of how the conversation would have gone:

The White House

I am being taken to a house.
Who's been taking you to a house?
I don't know — people I don't know.
How have you been getting there?
They drive me.
And you go? You go away with strangers?
Yes.
Where do they take you?
I don't know.
Who are these people?
I don't know.
And what do they do to you when you get there?
They give me sweeties.
What do you have to do for the sweeties?
Nothing.
Do they touch you?
No.
Do they say bad things to you?
No.
Do they do anything to you?
They make me play games.
Do they touch you or hurt you?
No.
What do they do after they've given you sweets and got you
    to play?
They take me back home.

It sounds like a story. It sounds made up. I'm sure that most people would think that, if strangers took the risk of luring a little girl into their car and taking her away for hours on end, they would do a damn sight more than give her some toffee and make her play piggy-in-the-middle. They were very clever in what they did and how they worked.

This lack of abuse in the white house would change. Some of the pseudo-religious things that happened there would be reflected elsewhere, so there were clearly links. I don't believe that anyone involved in any stage of my abuse was working alone; I believe that they all knew each other, and that they developed and shared a network of vulnerable children over the years. They were clever – and I was just something for them to play with.

CHAPTER 12

WHY WOULD ANYONE BELIEVE ME?

Adults really are a pain
to children such as I.
People maybe wonder,
So this poem will tell you why.

The 'innocent' nature of the parties soon changed.

There had always been strange things about the white house. Of course, the whole set-up was strange, but the robes threw me, as did the odd chanting which the grown-ups sometimes did. There was always low, unidentifiable music going on in the background. It sounded a bit like what you might hear in church, but it wasn't hymns. There were candles all over the place and a cloying smell that I later recognised as incense. It was like a church, but it wasn't a church. I had no idea that it was *their* church, a church they had made for themselves.

One day, we were playing games. There was always a slight twist to the games, as if you were only allowed to play it once you had accepted what the new rules were, and children were 'knocked out' when they had lost in some way (not necessarily the way we were used to). That day, I was knocked out. I only knew this because someone tapped me on the head and told me so. They also told me to get up and follow them.

I did exactly what I was told to do. I always did.

I followed a man into another room. There was another man already in there, he was wearing a suit. He looked perfectly ordinary, a straightforward guy wearing a suit on a Sunday. He wouldn't have stood out anywhere – people did dress up on the Sabbath back then.

The man who was already in the room was at the far end, to one side. There was a table in the middle, about four feet in length, with a coloured tablecloth on top. There was a crucifix at one end of the table.

'Get on the table, Lorraine,' the man told me. I wasn't scared but I couldn't quite get up. I turned round to the side a bit so that the first man could lift me onto it. I could lie flat without my head or feet hanging over; it seemed to be made for a child.

The first man told me that I had done well. He had a head teacher's tone of voice, it was very authoritative. He told me how to place my arms and that I needed to keep my feet on the table. I wasn't introduced to the guy who was at the top of the table. He was muttering something, something that sounded religious. I had no idea what it was, but it was similar to things I had heard in church.

While the man at the top of the table watched us – I

sensed he was in charge – the first one made the sign of the cross on my forehead. Then he told me to go back to the other room.

That was it.

Nothing else.

The first time I was taken into the room that was the only thing that happened. I remember thinking, 'What was that about?'

Initially, it seemed to me less involved than when my parents went to church. That would involve an hour at Sunday school, then hymns, and all of that, so I didn't see anything wrong in a bit of chanting. I was given a bag of sweets when I left that day, a whole bag to myself. Sweets were in short supply back then. That was the reward.

One Sunday at the white house, someone asked all of us children, as a group, whether we liked the parties. Of course, we said, 'Yes.'

'Are we all having fun?' he asked again. We nodded. 'Good,' he replied. 'If you want to keep coming, there is something you must do – you must be baptised,' he told us. 'Now, put your hand up if you want to be baptised.' Everyone did. We were getting fed every Sunday. No one did anything bad to us. If we didn't get baptised, it would stop. It was like Andrew's affection – if it had been taken away, that would have been awful. We were getting attention, food, games – all of which were alien to me. People were coming in and caring for me, picking me up, feeding me, playing silly games, taking me back. The thought of losing it was awful. I didn't want it to disappear, no one did.

Anyway, I thought, I was baptised already and that hadn't been a problem.

The following Sunday, we were all taken to the white house and given our robes to put on. We were reminded that the only way we could continue to come to the parties was to be baptised. No one had a problem with that. We were all put in various cars and vans and taken somewhere else. I think it was out of town as it took quite a while to get there. There was a boy in the van with me, but we didn't speak. Something in us, even then, made us realise that we shouldn't make allegiances. The adults in the front chatted quietly as we drove.

The place we arrived at was a sports club. It had a small indoor swimming pool which we could see immediately, and that was obviously where the baptisms would take place.

We were done one at a time. The kids were changed into different, fancier robes and one at a time we were got baptised. It was a complete immersion. There were steps down to the water where two guys waited. Someone else was saying some mumbo-jumbo at the side. It seemed odd but innocuous. I had to lie on my back in the water where one man caught me. I was told to relax then I was pushed under, very quickly. I couldn't make out any words.

It was very matter-of-fact, with nothing sexual; it was all very low-key and non-threatening. We went back into the changing rooms where some women helped us to get dried and changed, and then we went back to the white house for sandwiches and cake.

Why Would Anyone Believe Me?

I remember there was a party atmosphere about it that day, as if we'd achieved something, like getting a Brownie badge. It was a rite of passage. There was a sense of being part of something now, almost a gang.

Until the baptism, all it had been was a place where I was going, getting fed and playing silly games with some silly talk in the background. The first time I thought it was really 'churchy', for want of another word, was during the baptism. But it also changed things. I think they saw us as 'theirs' now.

There were new ways of talking to us. They were now calling us 'brother' and 'sister', and telling us to refer to each other that way, too. I became Little Sister and there was Brother Michael and Brother Peter and Sister Bernadette. They were all fake names, but it was about getting us to believe we belonged to them.

After the baptism, at the next meeting, they called the house 'the Kirk'. I was picked up in the van and there was already a boy in it. They told me he was 'Little Brother Jimmy' (he probably wasn't called that) and we were headed for the Kirk.

'You're very lucky,' the man driving told us. 'You're the special ones. You're the chosen ones.'

I didn't know if he meant Jimmy and me, or all of us. I didn't really care. They had never done anything to worry me, so I was still blasé about it all.

When we arrived at the house, the room where we used to play had been changed. There were chairs and a small altar, not the table full of food. There were adults already sitting on the chairs while we got changed into our robes. I noticed it was only the two of us. When Little Brother Jimmy and I were changed, we were led through to the altar, told to kneel, and given a drink. In hindsight, I know it was wine because it tasted funny, and things went woozy in my head very quickly. Getting us to drink would now become a common occurrence.

There was a man in colourful, elaborate clothes at the altar and there was lots of chanting going on around him. I could also make out the words this time:

The Lord is all seeing.
The Lord is all knowing.
The Lord is watching you.
The Lord knows your weaknesses.
The Lord wants you to be strong.

It went on for a while. It was hot and I felt dizzy. I knew I wouldn't be allowed to get up, so I stayed at the altar, feeling more and more disorientated.

I started to feel very sick, and someone must have noticed. Actually, I think they would have been looking out for it because I would have been given the wine deliberately for this purpose. If I was ill, I could be cared for. If I was cared for, I would feel safe. If I felt safe, they could ramp things up.

'Little Sister is unwell,' someone said. 'Send for the Mother.'

An older woman came towards me and took me in her

arms. She carried me to another room where she sponged my forehead and soothed me. Women were often used like this, I would come to realise. In the Kirk, they had traditional, caring roles. My own mother had never been like that – this was a novelty for me.

There was another man there, too, who continually said, 'Take care of Little Sister, Mother. She means a great deal to us. She is one of the chosen ones.' They made me feel very safe. Just as I was feeling a little better, the man passed me a goblet full of a red liquid. 'Drink this,' he said. I did. It made me feel worse.

'She needs to be bathed,' said Mother. 'Take Little Sister to the bathroom.'

A warm bath was drawn for me and I was treated with kindness. Mother washed me and cared for me. I felt like I belonged but, even then, I was always trying to keep something reserved as I could never trust anyone totally.

After I had been washed, I was taken back through to the original room. It looked as if no one had moved. I was led to the altar and the chanting began:

Thank you Lord for the return of Little Sister.
Thank you for the care you show your chosen ones.
Thank you for being all seeing.
Thank you for being all knowing.
We are in your debt, Lord.
We must never reveal your secrets, Lord.
We must do your work in silence, Lord.
We must never betray you.

I didn't trust those people; I didn't trust anybody. I wasn't making any investment that I didn't have to make. I realise now that all I was doing was getting what I needed from them. I was being fed and looked after – and if they were stupid enough to give it to me, then fine. I suppose I had an arrogance about myself. I had been abused so many times, there was a part of me that thought, 'I bet it is going to happen.' I fully expected it. To be honest, I remember being constantly surprised when it didn't. I don't know if that was done deliberately – raising my expectations. You get to the stage where you're waiting for something and if it doesn't happen, you wonder if you've got things wrong. It was a very difficult, confused time.

CHAPTER 13

INITIATION

There is no God
I just found out.
They lied to me.
I want to shout.

The comments at initiation about 'not telling' and 'secrets' were what I was expecting, really. I thought they would do something to me, and I was right. Nothing had happened up to that point because, of course, they were making absolutely certain that we wouldn't tell. If they had done more serious stuff sooner, then if we told at that point we could identify the house.

At the time I thought this is part of what I do now, I belong to this. It wasn't scary at all at first; it was just like going to another church and I had always liked church. Although I questioned why God hadn't helped me or stopped things I didn't like, I still had good memories of when I was little and I enjoyed Sunday school. Now, as part of this church, we belonged, we were special — given the sort of child I was, I didn't always believe that, but they were feeding me as well. I was accepting it superficially but there was also a part of me that wanted to belong. I wanted them to persuade me so that I could believe it. I wanted something. There was a big empty space inside me and I was desperate for something to fill it.

They were setting it up as a pseudo-religious sect and using those different elements to make us think that we belonged. I couldn't betray or tell because no one would believe me and also, I had sworn not to.

At the next visit to the Kirk, the initiation continued. When I was in my robe, there were more promises to be made:

I promise not to tell.
I promise not to betray the Lord.
I promise these things on my life.
I promise that I will keep my word.
I promise that I will keep the secret.

Andrew had never really pushed a need for secrecy onto me. He had groomed me so well that he didn't need to, but the others weren't so confident or so sure. They needed to be convinced that I understood, not just the consequences for them but for me and the future of my soul. If I 'told' then the battle could be compromised. It was important that I didn't show weakness by letting others know – the possible enemy – what was going on.

I was threatened that if I told, people would die. There

was no point threatening that my mum would die, because that wouldn't have bothered me, but I did care about my dad. And Uncle Andrew also said at one point, 'If you tell, they will kill me.' And I didn't want that to happen.

The dichotomy of the messages gradually got more and more complex. They would say things and we would repeat them. It didn't have huge meaning to me; I was going through the motions. The interesting thing is that I don't think I ever saw them touch any other child and I don't think any other child ever saw me being touched. They were clever.

I realised that being taken into the other room and lying down was all about compliance. You had to learn how to respond to commands, no matter what they were. At the second initiation meeting, I had no idea that it was all to become so much worse. The only thing which had ever been 'done' to me there was when I had been made to feel ill through the wine, but all that had happened after that was I was cared for by Mother.

It was all about to change.

I was taken through to the other room, where I had been told to lie on the table many times. When I got there, there was something new. There was a beautiful white dove in a gilded cage.

'Lie down,' I was told.

I did.

'Sit up,' I was told.

I did.

'You're the chosen one, Little Sister,' I was told. 'You're special. Do you accept that?'

I nodded.

'You've joined the brothers and sisters. You must not talk. You must understand that the Lord is all seeing and all knowing. Do you accept that?'

I nodded.

The man walked over to the cage and lifted the bird out. It was beautiful. I loved all animals and I longed to take this one in my own hands and stroke it. It looked so gentle, so soft and innocent.

'Lie down,' he told me. 'Lie down.'

I did.

He must have started squeezing the bird more tightly at that point, or perhaps the poor creature simply sensed something; whatever the reason, it began to squawk. It was panicking, and I was, too. I desperately hoped they wouldn't hurt it in any way.

The man stared at me while his hands got tighter and tighter around the dove. He twisted its neck right in front of me and I watched the light go out of its eyes. He took a knife and slit the bird open, then dipped his finger in and, with the blood of the dove still warm, drew a cross on my forehead.

'Your fault, Little Sister,' he said. 'Your choice.'

I'd seen dead things before, in those days death wasn't a great mystery, but it was awful to think that they had done this for me. I felt completely at fault; he was right, I was responsible for this.

Cruelty towards animals was something I could never get used to, but from that point on, it became quite common. They would often use birds and other creatures in their sacrifices and rituals, and, from that moment, I knew that they were well aware of how I felt about it. Even to this day, it is the cruelty against animals which sticks in my mind.

From that day, everything became more intense. I would be touched when I dressed and undressed. I would be touched through my own clothes and through my robes. They washed me when I got there, and they washed me afterwards – there was always sexual touching as part of that, but I also suspect they were getting rid of evidence. Both men and women would be involved. Although the women never seemed to be in positions of power and generally did the 'caring' activities, they also abused us when they wanted to.

By this stage, I was in too deep. If I'd told anyone before, what would I have said? If I told anyone now, they simply wouldn't have believed me. There was no way out. What I didn't know was that the white house, the Kirk, was just one more step on the ladder. Just as Andrew had prepared me, they were preparing me, too, and they began taking me to other places. They began taking me to parties which, I was told, were fun and which I was very lucky to be at. I didn't know whether my abusers were in charge of everything, or whether the other world – the world in which things were 'normal', like school, home, regular life – was the one which was superior. Sometimes Mum and Dad would be having a night out and Andrew would be babysitting when a car would turn up. Or there would be a change of plan while on the road to a picnic with Andrew. Or I would just be taken when I was playing on the street. They always seemed to know where I was if they wanted to find me. Often I would be met at the gates of my primary school – I guess they knew I wasn't going to talk by now. There were three different gates I could leave from, and I would sometimes try different ones, but I always felt that if it was a day they had decided to come for me, there would always be someone waiting at whichever gate I decided to leave from. They would tell me to get in the car, and I just would. I never really thought of saying 'No' or defying them, because I was so conditioned, even by that stage.

The stories I was told by them were always the same, but they didn't make any sense to me. It was as if they were all speaking from the same script but I didn't know what the purpose of it all was. Over and over again, they would say the same things:

You have to be strong.
You have to be tough.
You have to cope with things.
You have to deal with things.
You have to be stronger than anyone else.
Only certain people survive – if you want to survive, be
*   strong, be tough.*
Only the strong will survive.
Only the tough will get through this.
If you want to get through this, be strong, be strong, be
*   strong.*

There was something missing at the centre of all of this for me. What was it that I had to get through? What was I to survive?

As time went on, I realised that they thought – or they pretended to think – that there was a battle looming. This day of judgement approaching made sense of their fighting analogies and notions that warriors were being made, whose strength would be tested. However, I was just a little girl, a raped and abused little girl, terrified and alone. I had no concept of Satan or the Devil; I had no wish to be part of any imaginary ultimate conflict between good and evil. I just wanted someone to love me without hurting me.

It muddled my head so much. They said that I would hear stories at church about how the meek would inherit the earth but that I shouldn't be stupid enough to believe it because of course they wouldn't; the meek would inherit nothing. The strong survive; only the strong survive.

Was the truth that they were trying to convince themselves that the abuse they were inflicting was actually a preparation for what was to come? Had they convinced themselves that they were helping me by abusing me? They were making me strong; they were making me ready for the battle. If I could survive what they were doing to me, I would prove myself worthy to be on their side, and I would be everlastingly powerful.

The irony was that part of what they were telling me was true – you did have to be strong. If only I could make myself strong, I would think, if only I could make myself able to cope with the abuse, then maybe it would be easier.

If I could stop feeling, if I could accept what was being done to me, then maybe the hurt would stop.

Any abuse of any child is horrific, and abusers all mess with the heads of their victims, but this ... They were wrapping up what they did to me and trying to hide it, not just from society, not just from the authorities, but perhaps even from themselves. Did they not think of themselves as paedophiles, as abusers? I have often wondered whether they actually believed what they said. I don't think they did, but I can't put myself into the minds of people like that. I don't know what was all for show, what was just part of the act, and what was not.

I do know that they were cunning. By making this pretend battle seem like their primary concern, they were also making it unlikely that anyone would ever believe me if I did talk. The Devil? Satan? Making yourself strong for Judgement Day? Who would believe that, especially when it came from a nasty, unpleasant child who wasn't even loved by her own mother?

When I was seven, I ran away. It was the first of many attempted escapes. Initially, running was an impulsive thing. I didn't like life and I didn't want to be there. I wasn't suicidal, I just wanted out of what I was in. I hated the poverty and constant hunger. I loathed the feeling of not belonging. My plans were all about leaving, not about specifically going somewhere else. I just needed to get away. I didn't think any further forward than that.

One spring day, I sat in class and decided I would do it. I

would leave. I had to get out, but, really, I was running away from myself as much as anything or anyone else. When the bell went for break, I stood in a corner as usual, but when it rang again for us to go back in, I slipped behind a wall and waited. The playground emptied within minutes. I looked out and saw no one, so I ran. I didn't even get beyond the iron gates. I was spotted immediately – a teacher must have still been in the playground – and I was dragged back to class. There were lots of comments along the lines of 'What do you think you're doing?' but they didn't want me to answer them, they just wanted to let me know I'd be punished if it happened again.

I tried a few more times, but soon realised it didn't work. I'd need a different plan.

When I was eight, I waited until school had finished and went to the park. I still had no clear idea about where I was going, but, this time, I had the knowledge that no one would be looking for me for a while. Teachers were much more attentive than parents, in my eyes, and neither Mum nor Dad would even notice I was missing for ages. I didn't have anywhere to go, so when darkness fell, I was still in the park.

I must have been reported because, by the time I thought it was safe to come out and start making my way to goodness knows where, there were already police looking for me. I had barely got to the main road when I was picked up. They took me back home in a police car and I experienced the reaction of my mum which would turn out to be the same reaction every time this happened.

Our family was well-known and well-respected in our community, and the police only saw what they were shown. When they took me in, Mum acted like a real mother. She showed concern and she acted upset, as if all she wanted was to have her darling child back in her arms.

The police fell for it.

'Look what you've done!' the woman officer said. 'Your family is so upset and they've been so worried. You've done that! A good respectable family like yours and you're causing them such grief! Lots of children would do anything to have a lovely home like this! You've got your mum in such a state!'

'Oh, she has that,' said Mum, howling and wailing. 'I was terrified I'd never see her again. What if something had happened to you?' she asked in mock concern, clasping me to her chest. 'I'm so grateful that you found her officers, so grateful.'

The police gave me some more speeches about not worrying my lovely parents again and making sure I was a good girl in the future (I heard those words far too often), and then they left. They may have closed the door on a touching scene of a reunited mother and child, but they would barely be in their car before she started battering me.

The bruises lasted a while, and her words that night were the ones I'd hear many times.

How dare you do this?

You'll give this family a bad name with your behaviour.

Why are you like this?

We're a respectable family and you're an embarrassment.

Initiation

Don't you dare ever do that again.

But I did. I dared.

Every time it was the same. I'd run. I'd get found. I'd be taken back. I'd listen to the speeches. I'd be clasped in my mum's arms. I'd be left with her. I'd be punched and kicked senseless. And yet, by that time, she wasn't the one I was running from. There was so much in my own head that I needed to get away from. The abuse and the threat of abuse was constant. I had nowhere to go in my own mind or body. It was a living nightmare.

CHAPTER 14

TWO WORLDS

I am sad and bad and evil.
I don't care when you stare.
You don't see me.
Cause I'm not there.

I was so conditioned to the role of an abused person that I suspect I was giving out signals that I was a 'victim'. Other predators were noticing me, too. It was about this time that I was abused by a neighbour. He was just an opportunist, it wasn't linked to the other things which were going on, but his actions reinforced to me that abuse was all I was there for. It happened on a stairwell. The neighbour grabbed me, pulled my underwear down and attempted to rape me. He didn't manage completely, but he got quite far. I would never have thought of telling anyone because rape was just something that happened to me. Instead of telling someone about it, I avoided him; I took it as my responsibility to keep out of his way rather than thinking this was something grown men should not be doing to little girls.

145

It felt like I was living in two worlds. There was one world which was a daylight world and another dark world (though I'm not saying that everything bad happened in darkness because it didn't). In the daylight world, life had a veneer of normality – my mum was a bit violent, my dad was a bit distant, my big brother was in hospital somewhere, my little brother was always with Mum, and I had an uncle who was very loving and caring and did nice things for me. In this daylight world, I went to church and learned about Jesus. I was told about innocence and how He loves children.

Then there was the other side, the dark world, which was almost a mirror image. But what I was getting taught there was all of the opposites.

It was almost the reverse of Christianity. They would say that the Christian teachings were rubbish, and everything in the Kirk was right. They would sing a hymn – not one like 'All Things Bright and Beautiful' but something about being strong. The hymns were quite Germanic, with harsh, aggressive chanting. They were always about power and strength and right. When they were singing I would be standing or sitting with whoever had taken me.

There was a hierarchy among the men – and obviously the kids weren't privy to any decision-making. We would be told one thing but then, in order to retain even more power, it would turn out not to be true. I'd be told that we were going to Jimmy's and so I would be prepared in my mind for what had happened at Jimmy's previously, the type of abuse, where it was, but then we would end up somewhere else and 'Jimmy' wouldn't be the Jimmy from before. Sometimes I would be told we were going to a nice, fun party for Hallowe'en but there would be nothing to do with Hallowe'en when we got there or it would be the wrong time of year.

There was nothing you could be sure about, it was all lies, and it was all done to mess with minds because the control and the power trip was so important to them, as well as it being necessary in terms of screwing up anything you might remember from an evidential perspective.

They would also build up your hopes, in terms of any tiny thing you did like or were less scared of, so I'd be told that it would be a nice night because Uncle Andrew would be coming, but then it wouldn't be him. There would be someone else who I was told was my Uncle Andrew as he was raping me. Sometimes, this other person would have a mask on but I would know that it wasn't really him. They would be the wrong height or the wrong weight or, sometimes, even obviously a woman. There were occasions when I would be told to call the person Uncle Andrew and then when I did, they would ask me why I was doing that. Sometimes he really would be there, too, but that was rare.

Was it Satanic? I don't know.

Personally I don't believe in God or Satan or any of those things, but abusers use whatever they can to silence children because if you go to the police and say something about Satan, you are so much less likely to be believed. I personally think they were just a group of like-minded people who had no beliefs other than that they wanted to get satisfaction out of abusing children and it's as simple and horrible as that.

My uncle certainly doesn't have any satanic beliefs – he just thinks that he loves children and is allowed to get sexual satisfaction from them. Why is there sex involved if it is just about Satan? Why does it always come down to them getting off? No matter what they do that's all it is, whether masturbation or penetration or humiliation, that's what it's about. I encountered people who just liked to humiliate – they wouldn't allow you to go to the bathroom, you would be given drink after drink, fizzy drinks, whatever, so you ended up absolutely desperate and that's where they got off – that's when they started to masturbate themselves, as you stood there peeing yourself. That was just awful, so humiliating. Where is God or Satan in that?

Writing this book has brought back such strong memories, such as lying in bed as a child, asleep, and being woken by someone I didn't know whispering, 'You must be strong.' Who were these people? How did they get into the house? I can only assume that it happened on nights when my parents were out and Andrew was babysitting.

Andrew introduced me to most of the people who abused me, but I also recognised some of them. At least one was a neighbour, and there were a few occasions when I would wake to the horror of someone's hands under my bedclothes, look at their face, and know exactly who they were. As the hands and fingers slid under the blankets, it would be the same old message – be strong, the strong survive.

So, I just had to take it. I had to take the horror and the abuse and the rape and the torture and the degradation.

Everyone involved in my abuse was always very careful about evidence and witnesses, but that is the case, more often than not. Abusers are careful. They are cunning and they have many ways to make sure they are never found out, or that the children they abuse are never believed if they do tell. They are usually very sly people; they keep people separate.

The abusers who are most likely to get away with it are the ones you can't identify and the simplest way for them to do that is to put on a mask. Masks were frequently used when I was taken to group settings. They were usually animal masks, often horses, or other faces. Not only do the masks prevent the child from recognising their abuser but they also make it sound so much more fantastical if any child does tell. Not only are you reporting about sexual acts being carried out which no one wants to believe any adult could perpetrate on a minor, but you are also telling tales of masks and secrecy and houses that can't be identi- fied. Nothing can be pinned down. It's so much easier for anyone listening to dismiss the stories as fabrications than to believe them; and the people behind the abuse know that.

I was so young when all of this happened, but I had already been labelled as a horrible little girl, according to my family. I was unlovable and nasty. I didn't have friends and no one liked me. I was untrustworthy, I was dirty and unkempt. If a child like that starts talking of things which no one wants to hear, how on earth do you think she will be believed? The things that were being done to me were awful – there was oral sex and masturbation, there was rape and sacrifice. Who would want to accept that it was going on? Who would listen to a difficult child who told such tales?

The abuse became standard in my life. And it wasn't just men who were abusing me now, there were also women. In the late 1950s and early 1960s, this would have been one of the hardest things of all for someone else to believe. When Myra Hindley's involvement in the Moors Murders hit the headlines, one of the most appalling things for people to accept was the fact that a woman had been involved. In the minds of the public, the stereotypical woman was nurturing and caring; she loved children and went out of her way to keep them from harm. I knew that wasn't always the case from my own home experience but, to begin with, I had thought that other women weren't like that. After all, I had seen other mums be nice to their kids. When women became involved in the group abuse, it confused me but, after a little while, nothing surprised me.

I was in a messed up life. The things they told me about the most powerful people being the winners was something I could actually see on a daily basis. I had been to church and I had tried to ask God for help – but it was all useless and they reinforced that belief in me all of the time. They said they had power and they did. They never got found out, no one told on them – all of the things they said were self-per-petuating. I wasn't the only one keeping quiet, we all were.

They said that if I told, they would kill me. I believed them. Why wouldn't I? Everything else they had said was true, so why would they lie about this? I hated the world I lived in, but I felt that it was me who was wrong to feel like this and not that they were wrong.

The horrors of the world supported them. Television was becoming more popular and, even there, all I could see was violence and fighting. Films showed the same. News was coming through about what had really happened with the Germans and to Japanese prisoners of war. We were told about the concentration camp atrocities. All of the messages were the same. The powerful succeed. Bad things happen. You have to be on the winning side.

The other thing which I realised was that my life wasn't necessarily worse than that of many other people. I heard radio reports about Auschwitz and I felt grateful for my life at times. As a whole, society was telling us how lucky we were in those post-war years. We had food (although I didn't always), we lived in a democracy, we went to school and we were free. If this was all the case, I was the one who was wrong. If I couldn't work out how to fit in, it was entirely my fault.

This must just be the way the world worked – that I couldn't fit in, that I questioned things and hated what was happening, was my fault. Again.

CHAPTER 15

TYPICAL

No one hears me cry inside
Is God another lie?

One day, I was taken in a car to a house and told to go inside. I had never seen it before and, as usual, I didn't know where it was. We had driven for about twenty minutes, but I had been on the floor with a blanket over me, so had no idea about the area or location of the place we arrived at.

'Get out of the car. Go in that house. Stay there.'

The voice was gruff and there was no conversation. Commands were simply barked at me.

I did as I was told. I always did as I was told.

The door wasn't locked and as I pushed it gently, it swung open. I walked in and there was a room to my left and the door was also open. In there were four men and two women. I couldn't see one of the women, but I could hear two different female voices. There was the usual, weird music playing, the tunes which always played and sounded mournful and religious. People were talking

153

among themselves. No one looked at me as I walked in; it was as if it was the most natural thing in the world for a little girl to be dropped off at the door of a house and wander into a room full of strangers. They didn't look at me or talk to me to begin with and, as usual, I just stood there, waiting for instructions, completely obedient and passive.

Eventually, someone, a man, said, 'Go over there and sit on that couch.' I moved over towards it and felt as if I was going to vomit. I could smell the sofa as soon as I got close. It had the most awful, disgusting stink coming off it. It was a combination of damp and bodily fluids and even the sick that I thought was going to come from me. I can still remember it – sometimes you latch onto the strangest memories, not always the things which were done to you, but the 'accessories' or the surroundings.

'Sit!' someone snapped. I did. I had no choice. It looked horrible, it smelled horrible, but I could no more have refused than I could have run to the police. A man came over and sat beside me. I recognised him; he was a regular. There was no preamble in this setting. As soon as he sat on the couch, he began touching me. I was wearing leggings and a top, and his hands were all over me through the fabric. Did I protest? No. No, I didn't. I had been groomed for this, after all. It was what I was there for. I was nothing more than entertainment. I was in no position to do anything to stop what happened to me in any of these scenarios.

'Take your trousers off,' he said. At that point, I froze. I was used to being passive so performing a decisive action like that was beyond me. I was so used to having things done to me that it was as if all free will had gone. However, to them, as the seconds passed, it must have looked as if I was defying him. I wasn't. I just didn't have the energy or impetus to do anything. If he had removed my trousers, I wouldn't have resisted, but the very fact that he was asking me to do something wasn't registering in my brain. I had locked myself away from all that I knew would be happening.

All hell broke loose.

He leapt to his feet and all of the other men in the room stood up. They had been watching what was happening on the sofa; they had been expecting a show, I suppose. The whole atmosphere changed to one of anger and disgust – at me. The man who had been sitting beside me slapped my face, and then, one by one, the others joined in. There was a constant stream of adults hitting me, before I was pinned to the floor. It all happened so quickly. There was a man holding down each of my arms and two others holding my legs. They pulled my clothes off then spreadeagled me, each holding a limb and pinning me there like a star.

Others hit me and nipped me. They were in a frenzy. It was as if they all needed to get to me – people, men and women, were stretching their arms into the melee, and if they couldn't get a good swing at me, they would resort to tiny, almost playground, attacks with their nails, scratching and pinching.

I didn't know what to do, and I'm not sure they did

either, because I was suddenly dragged up and thrown to the sofa. Whatever was to happen to me, it was as if the floor wasn't a restricted enough area – there were too many people trying to assault me at once, even for those who were attempting to control the dynamics of my attack. I was shoved onto the stinking sofa once more, naked, and raped by the man who I had been perceived as defying.

I tried to struggle, of course I did – but it was impossible. There were so many of them holding me, and I was no match for them, or for the baying group in the background who cheered my rapist on. They were shouting all the time, all of them. This shouting, these insults, did not take the form you might perhaps expect them to. They weren't sexual insults, as such (although obviously they were all getting some degree of sexual gratification from what was occurring); no, they were the same old taunts which were always used. I was stupid. I was worthless. I was wicked.

The noise was overwhelming and lots of the words were mixed up.

Finally I was dragged off the sofa and thrown to the floor again. I was hurting a lot. The earlier physical attacks were now compounded by the pain of being raped. But I felt as if I was watching what was happening from afar and so I couldn't quite believe my own reaction when I started screaming.

This was the first time I had ever done this. I had always been quiet; I had always taken everything. So I don't know where my voice came from. All of a sudden, I was aware of one of the women standing over me with a glass jug. She began pouring cold water onto my head. It went in my mouth, it went up my nose, it was choking me; I kept trying to move my head and she kept shoving me to make sure the water was hitting me. It went on for such a long time.

Until then I had thought that Andrew's betrayal had been the most awful thing in my life, but this was worse. I really thought I was going to die. I could hear, in the background, the other woman shouting something and then things trickled through – you're the Devil's child, the Devil's child. I'd heard that before, usually in connection with being left-handed. In those days, teachers would try to make me write with my 'right' hand. When I reached for a pencil, I would get hit with a ruler to try and stop me using my left hand. I was even examined by a doctor as it was seen as a medical anomaly. The doctor said that I was strongly, completely and utterly left-handed, and should be left alone. However, it had always stuck in my mind that this was another way in which I was different from other people. Andrew knew that Mum screamed at me whenever she noticed I was using my left hand, so he made sure that he was warm in his tone when he would 'lovingly' tease me for being different, for having different ways – again, it was a way of bonding me to him. However, he, too, had said it was a sign of the Devil, so when, in this setting, I heard them all saying I was the Devil's child, they weren't saying anything I hadn't heard before. They were just confirming what had already been shouted at me and whispered to me.

Everything started to blend in with the music – it was as

157

if they were chanting it: Devil's spawn, Devil's spawn, Devil's spawn. My head wasn't there. I remember realising that I needed to get away, and telling my body that I needed to get away, but I couldn't do it. I physically couldn't do it. There wouldn't have been anywhere to go anyway, but that was one of the few occasions when I actually thought that getting away was my best option. I was more scared of staying than of running, but my body couldn't do it.

Naked, shaking and terrified, I lay there as they all fed from me. They fed from my fear – I am sure that was what they all found sexually exciting. Of course, some of them actively wanted to sexually abuse a small child, but there were others who never touched me but who seemed thrilled and on the verge of orgasm by what was happening.

The man who had raped me was walking back and forth, working himself up into a frenzy. 'We will clean you! We will clean you!' he shouted each time he passed by my shivering body. 'You are filth! You are a filthy child, but we will clean you! We will cleanse your body and your soul. We will cleanse you of all filth! We will clean you!'

The others began to join in his chant.

I guess they had an excuse if they believed their own lies. If they convinced themselves that I was dirty, that I was the filthy one, then they could also convince themselves that they were using the water to clean me.

I doubted it, though. It was all just an excuse.

I started to choke. I was in a terrible state of confusion. And then, suddenly, a man stopped the water and said, 'It's fine, everything will be fine.'

The relief was immense and, of course, there was a degree of gratitude in there, even though this man was one of the ones who must have been involved in it all and, therefore, was partly responsible for what had happened to me in the first place. It didn't matter, I was grateful.

'Everything will be fine now,' he kept saying, soothingly. 'I'll look after you, won't I? Your Uncle Andrew will look after you.'

He wasn't my Uncle Andrew.

He kept saying that he was as he wrapped me in a blanket, and I kept shivering with fear and shock.

'See?' he kept repeating. 'Your Uncle Andrew wouldn't let anything happen to you. I'll look after you, I'll make everything fine. Good old Uncle Andrew!'

He led me to the bathroom, all the while saying that he was my uncle, and I really, really wished he was. My Uncle Andrew loved me and looked after me, and that was all I wanted.

'I rescued you,' the man said as he ran the bath. 'You just need to be a good girl again, then it will all be fine.'

He told me to get in the bath and he started to clean me, washing me gently and with care. As I lay in the water, I became braver about opening my eyes. I did feel a little safer. I looked at the man more carefully. He wasn't Andrew, but I did know him. He was a neighbour of my uncle's, one of the people who had, on some occasions, been involved in abuse, but this was the first time I had seen him that day.

The man kept cleaning me and kept muttering that he

had to make sure I was properly clean. For this, it seemed, he had to spend a great deal of time washing between my legs. I was numb to it all. So much had happened that I barely even registered the continued abuse. He also apologised because the thing he went on to dry me with was rough, it was like sacking.

I started shaking uncontrollably and I couldn't talk. He dressed me and kept saying it would all be fine; then he took me through to the horrible couch in the living room again.

That was awful for me. I could smell it, just as bad as it had been the first time. I felt a choking sensation in my throat. Everything was coming back, everything.

'I can't ... I can't ...' I said, struggling to talk. I just couldn't bring myself to sit there, knowing that it had been my reaction on that couch that had started it all off.

The man looked at me as the words caught.

'Never mind,' he said. 'Come over here, this'll be better. Come over here with Uncle Andrew.' He took me by the hand to an armchair in the corner of the room. 'Now then,' he said, 'you're awfully upset. Let's just get you calmed down. Everything will be fine now you're with your Uncle Andrew.'

The chair smelled just as bad as the couch. He sat with me on his lap, and he rocked me until I began to calm down. Over and over again he whispered, 'It'll be OK, really, it'll be OK.' He was kind, but I was still suspicious. I knew it could turn, I knew he could turn.

After a while, he asked, 'Would you like to go home now?'

I nodded, wondering if this was a trap, too, but he got up

160

out of the chair with me and took me outside to a car. He dropped me a few streets from my house and reminded me not to tell anyone; as if I needed reminding. Anyway, who would believe what had just occurred?

I couldn't predict what would happen from one day to the next. It was a hideous existence, and I was still slap bang in the middle of it.

CHAPTER 16

GAMES DAY

I am nine and I am mine,
Not yours or yours or yours.
Only mine. Just me alone.
Made of stone.

I was taken back to that house a few more times, but I never complained. I never reacted again. I was a quick learner; who wouldn't be when those were the sort of lessons dished out? From that time on, I never screamed, and if someone told me to do something, I did it without question.

I continued to be picked up from outside school or on the street. It wasn't regular, in that I didn't know it would always be a Monday, or it would always be at four o'clock, but I knew there was always the potential.

They started to use even more locations. There was an old schoolhouse not far from me which was boarded up and unused (apart from by them), and I was also taken to some buildings in the countryside. Every time, from then on, I wasn't allowed to sit on a seat in the car. I was too

163

'wicked', so I had to lie on the floor. I was still being called 'Devil's child', as well. That was pretty much their pet name for me.

They had also started to call me different names. Although they knew that I was Lorraine, they would say that I was Mary, or Elizabeth. It was as if my given name didn't meet with their approval. Names started to be blurred all of the time. The man who had claimed to be my uncle must have been told to say that by someone. It was, I suppose, partly a way of confusing me with regards to identities if I had ever told anyone, but I think that the psychological aspect of it was what they liked more than anything. Your name is your identity in many ways; if they messed with that, you had absolutely nothing to hold on to. What they didn't know was that I would finally take some power from it. Just as I had won tiny victories against my mother and my granny's cruelties, I would do so with this.

The worst thing about the confusion with the names was that I had to act as if they were telling the truth. It became more and more common for other people to claim they were Uncle Andrew. They would call each other by his name, or say that he was coming to see me, and it wouldn't be him. It was as if what they were doing to me physically and emotionally wasn't enough for them; they wanted to make me collude with their mind games, too.

Prior to the schoolhouse, I remember being taking out into the countryside one day but I counted 'left, right' in my head, as I lay on the floor. I don't know why I did this as I wasn't going to tell, but I lay there trying to remember that it was 'ten seconds then left turn, five seconds, then another left turn, twenty seconds, then a right turn'. I would keep it going in my head – perhaps to keep myself sane.

The car door opened and I was told to get out. There were lots of adults waiting there, as always, but I was shocked to see other children, too. Although there had been kids at the first house, where the initial meetings had taken place, I had thought, since then, that there was no one else. That somehow, and for some reason, I had been chosen alone. I was always being told that I was wicked and that I was the Devil's child, so I am sure that I believed this was why these things were happening to me. It hadn't occurred to me that there were more wicked children, more spawn of the Devil, and it had certainly never occurred to me that we would all meet up at some point.

I stood there, waiting for instructions. There wasn't a bone in my body which was willing to do something of its own accord. It all had to come from them. I had learned that lesson.

The adults were all standing around in a group, too, and then, suddenly, someone shouted, 'Right, let's have some games.'

I knew this wouldn't be fun. There would be no laughter or enjoyment or spontaneity, and it would all have been planned far in advance. The adults would know exactly what they wanted out of this and I would just have to wait and see.

'Races!' someone else called. 'Let's start with races!'

The children had all been brought to this play by someone different, 'their' adult, as it were, and they were now led by their adult to a starting line. There were six others, boys and girls. We all kept our heads down. We were all isolated in our own bubbles. Some of the children were bigger than I was, some were smaller. Some of them I would see again, some would disappear. I don't know where they got them from. I can only guess that there were more children like me than I had ever suspected. The streets must have had a lot of lost souls whose parents kicked them out in the morning and never gave a moment's thought to where they went for the rest of the day.

We were in a sort of field, with a farm building at one end, and lots of old, dumped and dilapidated bits and bobs lying around. They lined us up and told us where the finishing line was. It was at some random point where two men were holding a rope.

'The winner will get a prize!' announced a woman at the side of us all. 'Try your hardest! Try to win!'

I was never a great runner, but I did what I could and I didn't lose. I ran my heart out and I was glad of that, for the little boy who lost was punished as soon as the others crossed the line and the 'winner' was taken off for his prize. The rest of us were left standing there, not knowing what would happen next, but absolutely certain that we would do all we could never to lose or win, just stay in the middle and be invisible if possible.

'More games! More games!' shrieked a woman after a few moments. 'Come on, let's have more games!'

The children had no enthusiasm. We all knew this wasn't natural or normal. We followed a woman to a grassy part of the farmyard and she told us to sit down in a circle.

She looked over at a group of other adults as if waiting for an invisible sign, then nodded at them and said, 'Send a Letter.' I knew this game, we played it at school. It usually involved one child skipping round the group and then choosing another child to chase them. 'I sent a letter to my love and on the way I dropped it ...' It's a happy game with a happy tune. I knew that wouldn't be the case here.

I realised that one child must have been told to start as I had the sense of someone running round. Someone then shouted, 'Drop the letter and choose!' When the letter was 'dropped', rather than chasing their friend, as would be usual, the second child was taken away, put to the side and the group was reduced. I was one of the chosen children at one point, and I stood to the side. The game kept going until there was a winner, who would be taken away just as the running winner had been.

That day, the main lesson to be learned was that I didn't want to lose. If you were a loser, you'd get punished. There was so much violence, but never the sound of a single tear being shed. I remember always trying to work out what was the best angle. I soon worked out that day that, although they said the winners would get a prize, it was usually a lie. The 'prize' might be something horrific, too. None of the children spoke, so when the winners returned they didn't tell us what went on when they were taken away. I decided to have the same strategy as I had at school; stay in the middle, don't draw attention to myself. I didn't lose and I didn't win. I couldn't risk either of those options.

As the 'games' went on, the messages that were being passed on to us were the same as usual. 'Be strong.' 'Only the strong survive.' 'Don't be a loser.' I was getting sick of the sound of all that, because it wasn't only being drummed into me in the context of the abuse, but it was all around me in normal life, too. The country wasn't that long out of a war, and people still had that mentality. Everywhere, on the radio, in school, there were the same messages promoting the virtues of strength and power. Andrew had said similar things to me from the start because of his Army background. It was all I ever heard.

This must have happened in spring or summer, because the weather was fine and the outdoors abuse happened more. On that first day of 'games', I wasn't sexually abused, but I suspect others were, those who had won or lost races and were taken away. I remember a whole series of trips to outdoors locations where 'games' would always take place.

I have so many questions about those times, but I know they'll never be answered. However, it doesn't stop me asking them and I'd bet that every single person reading this will be asking the same things.

Who were these people? Well, I know that my uncle was involved, and I know that there were some individuals who I would see at other times, such as neighbours or, on one occasion, a teacher who I recognised when I was older. However, knowing who some of them were doesn't help me to understand any of the other questions.

How did they get together and how did they ever find such like-minded souls? Again, I have no idea. There were no mobile phones in those days to organise meetings. There were no personal computers to contact people. There was no Facebook to set up things between those who had the same 'interests'. The only ways people could communicate were by post, by phone (usually public phones in phone boxes if you were working class), or in person. So, how did they ever find each other? I don't know whether there was some initial link – perhaps they knew each other through church or even worked together. If that is how it all came about, how on earth did it progress, though? You can't exactly go up to someone and ask whether they like to abuse children and enquire whether they would like to come to a deserted farmyard to watch them being tormented, can you?

One thing which can't be disputed is that like-minded people have always managed to find ways to identify and meet others. Sometimes these groups come together because their behaviour or activities are frowned upon or illegal in society at that time, even though there is nothing dangerous or damaging about what they do. People always find a way to meet, to identify who thinks the same way, and who will be a friend rather than foe, and I can only assume that the people who were behind my childhood terrors were no different in this regard.

In addition to this, there are always people who

manipulate. There would, undoubtedly, be certain key people among that group, some who were leaders and others who were followers. I certainly saw individuals who never really took part in anything, and also some who looked as if they didn't want to be there, so it doesn't take a huge leap to wonder whether there were elements of blackmail going on – once someone gets into a set up like that, how do they ever get out?

There would, no doubt, be different aspects of the network which appealed to different people. There would be those who would be there for the sexual side of the abuse, and those who would be drawn to anything which allowed them to control others or exploit weakness. There would be those who would relish power in any situation and those who would follow, due to the charisma of others and the weakness of their own characters.

Another question which could be asked is, where did they get their ideas from? How did they come up with the tortures and degradations which they inflicted on the children in their control? This was a time long before the Internet, so there were fewer images and less mental stimuli in an obvious sense. However, people who have these desires need only use their imaginations. They may very well have had thoughts and actions sparked by something they read or saw but, even in a world where no such things existed, someone who has the twisted need to humiliate and abuse children will act out what they want, irrespective of whether they have seen a picture or read a book which shows the same activity.

There were many elements in the abuse, but I can only guess at what influences were behind what they did. Certainly there were perversions of 'traditional' church ceremonies and activities, and it may have been that some of the protagonists came from a religious background. They may have been building on what they knew or, if they were against such practices, they may have been intent on ridiculing what others believed in. The races and sports activities may have existed because one, or more, of the abusers worked in a school or educational capacity and they were acting out their own fantasy of what they wanted to see at these events; or it could have been an attempt to reclaim an event in which they had been ridiculed as a child.

The use of animals and 'props', of robes and of stage-managed sacrifices, could have come from Aleister Crowley or Dennis Wheatley books, from the developing counter-culture which was spreading from North America, from the use of psychedelic drugs which were, again, spreading throughout the 1960s. There is a possible explanation for everything – and a conclusive answer to nothing at all.

CHAPTER 17

MY WEAKNESS

There is no good
There's only bad.
They made it up
To turn me mad

When I was next taken away, they wanted me to fight someone. It was a girl. She was much bigger than I was, but I knew that I would have to do it. I couldn't hide with these fights because I didn't have control; it wasn't up to me whether I got chosen. As soon as I was taken to the old schoolhouse, I was picked. I knew I would be at some point; it was one of the only certainties I had felt for a long time.

Shoved into the centre of the fighting ring, I heard cat-calls of 'loser' and 'weakling' all around me. From the moment they told us to begin, I went for her. I was like an animal. I was possessed. The poor child didn't stand a chance. This was me fighting for my life and they had finally made me realise that I had to do anything; I would do anything, to survive.

I was horrified by how vicious I was that day, and I found that I would do things I never thought I was capable of. I quickly got the girl on to the ground and, as I lay on top of her, kicking and punching like a wild beast, I reached over and grabbed a stone. Without a moment's hesitation, I pummelled her head and her face with it. In my mind – distorted as it was – this was the only way I could guarantee my win. She could have got up at any point, I reasoned, and I would lose. I would be raped again. I couldn't risk that, so I gave up what little humanity I had left and attacked that girl with every ounce of energy I had left in my body.

I was left with a huge sense of shame. I still carry that. It was so out of character for me, but I lost a part of me that day. I was commended for it by them. Finally, I had done something they approved of. At last, I was part of the group. I was so confused about what was right and what was wrong. I got praise when I did what they said was correct. Hitting another child was right. Hitting back was right. These are all the messages I now oppose in my work, so it has stayed with me – just not in the way they planned or hoped.

Up until then, although there had been other children taken to the same places as me, I hadn't been a witness to their abuse, and they hadn't been a witness to mine. That changed. They must have now been so convinced that I – and the others – wouldn't tell that they didn't care about us seeing everything. They must have groomed us all individually and then, when they felt it was safe, they brought us together. It was like a perverted training academy, and I had graduated.

My Weakness

There were never any other children in the cars with me, though. We were all brought separately to wherever the abuse was to take place but, once we got there, we were allowed to be with the others. There was nothing positive in this. I had been so indoctrinated, so broken, that I couldn't look or connect with any other child. They were the same. There was no eye contact; there were no attempts to talk. You had to look after yourself; you had to save your own skin at all costs. That was the horror and the inhumanity of what they had reduced us to.

We weren't always taken to deserted places. Sometimes the farms they took us to were clearly working establishments. There would be animals around, there would be machinery, and I could even hear work going on. I don't know how that was facilitated. Was the farmer part of the group of abusers? Did he know what was happening? Was it simply done for money? Had someone been paid to ask no questions? Still the questions were there, still the answers were not.

When things happened in a place which was obviously still in use, then the races and games and fights occurred indoors and they would use whatever was around as part of the abuse. I had two weaknesses. The first – my abhorrence of violence – had been broken by them. The second was my love of animals. I was a fool to think that they wouldn't use it against me. There are chapters of my abuse which I simply can't revisit – and which I am unwilling to inflict on anyone else. What had happened with the dove in the white house had been bad enough, but there was much worse to come and I shudder to this day when I think of how I was punished for my love of animals. Those times were hard. What had been done to me, personally, by everyone who abused me was appalling but, for me, the cruelty inflicted on innocent animals was even worse. If I ever spotted an animal on the farms we were taken to, they homed in on it and anything done to that creature was always my fault. It was my need, my longing for love and affection, which put them in danger and was, as such, another indicator of my weakness.

Around about this time, they also started making a fuss about our birthdays. The twist, of course, was that it wouldn't actually be anyone's real birthday when we were forced into celebrating it, but there would be a party nonetheless.

One day, it was the 'birthday' of a boy who seemed a lot younger than me. I didn't really recognise him. None of us looked at each other, remember, and there were so many different people around that it was hard to keep track. There was a table set up with paper plates and cups, but no food. The food was brought out by some of the adults on other plates – it was as if it had all been pre-prepared. They placed these down on top of the empty plates.

'Eat it quickly!' we were told. 'Don't waste time! Quickly! Quickly!'

On the plate was rice, and what I thought was some sort of vegetables. We were give spoons and told to be fast, otherwise we'd be losers. I did as I was told; or I tried to. As I started eating, I realised there was something wrong, very wrong, with the food.

It didn't smell right.

It didn't taste right.

It was moving.

Food shouldn't move.

What I'd thought was rice wasn't rice at all. It was maggots.

I started to retch and someone noticed. There was always someone watching everything, and they would have hoped one of the children was going to react this way.

'Stop it! Don't be sick!' I was told. 'Only the weak can't do what is asked of them! Keep eating.'

I couldn't. I had to be sick. I could feel the maggots crawling in my mouth and now that I knew what they were, the thought of them in my stomach made me vomit violently.

'No! Don't do that!' People were screaming at me. One of them picked up my spoon and scraped all of my sick onto the plate. 'Eat it. Eat it all.'

I looked at the faces of my tormentors and knew I would have to do this. I put a spoonful into my mouth but it just came straight back up again as soon as it hit my throat.

The person who had scraped it off the ground the first time moved to do so again, but someone stopped him. 'No, don't do that,' she said.

Thank God, I thought, because I could think of nothing worse.

'She can pick it up herself. Go on, Susan,' she said. 'Pick up your food. Eat your food. Enjoy your delicious food.'

I had to. I scraped my own maggot-crawling vomit off the dirt and put it on my plate, and then, somehow, I forced every mouthful down. I gagged constantly and, at times, I had to be held down, but it was done.

This was a theme of the parties – the food was always something which should never be eaten. For many years, whenever I saw rice, I would look for movement. Unsurprisingly, I'm fussy with food to this day.

At another party, there was a pie.

The pastry looked fine; it all seemed and smelled fine. By then, we'd been tricked a few times, but there is always hope.

Once we'd eaten it, we were asked, 'Did you enjoy that?' We all nodded – even if we hadn't, we'd have still nodded. 'Good,' we were told. 'Plenty more where that came from – there are always plenty of stray dogs around, after all.'

Was it dog? I have absolutely no idea. I believed it was, and that was what they wanted. They just wanted to mess with our heads.

Food, from that point, became an increasing problem. I realised later that this was where the crossover with the other group was found: both groups used food as a means of control – the first used it to lure children in; the other to torture and play mind games.

No matter what I was faced with, I did it – I had been trained well, by Andrew and by the people at the first house. If someone said stand up, I stood up. If they said take

your clothes off, I took my clothes off. If they said eat maggots, I ate maggots.

When I heard other children in school talking about parties, I couldn't understand why they seemed excited. For
me, it was all about more abuse. I honestly thought that all
children were going through the same as me, but that they
were strong so they liked what was happening. So much felt
wrong, but I was told that was my fault, it was me who was
wrong, everybody else was fine with it. I thought of my
own weaknesses and they seemed more pronounced. In my
mind, there was clearly something wrong with me because
I didn't like it – this was getting reinforced by everything
they told me.

I was so at odds with everything. I didn't fit in anywhere.
The only hope for me – I was told – was to be fixed. My
abusers could fix me if I worked with them. If I did everything I was told and didn't disobey, then maybe there was a
chance for me.

There would be times when everyone – everyone in the
real world, the daylight world – would be celebrating something, and these times became important to my abusers.
Their control of every event meant that they could impose
their own interpretation on it. The times didn't always coin-
cide but there would be some link. They would use
everyday objects and associations to normalise what they
were doing. For Hallowe'en, the adults would dress up and
they would sometimes dress the kids up, too. Sometimes,
there would even be a fun atmosphere to start with. It was

so confusing, because at school we were given masks and we would have Hallowe'en decorations, too, so if that part of the festivities was normal, then maybe the other things that went on were normal, too. I didn't know where the boundaries were. I could even see the decorations that they used at our parties at school and at the abuse locations being sold in shops, so, perhaps, it really was acceptable. I would go to the parties, though, and see the decorations but the atmosphere would be totally different. What should I believe?

The games for Hallowe'en were just the same at the abuse locations as at school – at both places I was encouraged to bob (or 'dook') for apples. The only difference during the abuse was that the adults would hold our heads down under the water until they judged we could barely take it anymore. Just when we thought we would drown, they would let us bob up. We would all sit there watching it happen to the other kids, knowing it would be our turn soon, knowing that no one would get out of it, and having to accept it as fate.

They thought all of this was great fun. There was always laughter when this type of thing happened. Some of them were drunk, but all of them were having a good time. I never saw drugs being used, but that isn't to say they weren't. In fact, looking back on it as an adult, I'd be very surprised if they hadn't used drugs.

There were occasions when they dressed up in a terrifying manner. On one occasion, there were 'witches' chasing children around a room and handing them over to warlocks.

My Weakness

Within this, I was told to take part in a game of hide and seek. 'RUN!' screamed a witch. 'Run for your lives! Hide before you're caught! The weak will be caught and handed over, and there will be no escape!'

It may sound corny to you reading this, but I can assure you it didn't feel that way. These were people who had absolutely no scruples when it came to hurting children; I was living proof of that. If they told me to run and hide, that's what I would do.

Some of them were dressed as ghosts, too, and they would all try to find us. This game was once played in the woods and you could always tell when they had found a child – I remember hearing triumphant shouts from the adults when they had tracked someone down. That day, in the woods, I wondered if I could get right through the trees and out the other side. Maybe I could just keep going. Perhaps they would never find me. Hardly. They caught me within seconds of me even having the thought.

For Hallowe'en, there would also be bonfires which they would dance around, shrieking and chanting, calling up all sorts of demons from their imaginations. The autumn and winter dark would have come early at those times, and it would only be late afternoon but the sky would be black and it was easy for them to whip up an atmosphere of menace. In some ways, it was harder to cope when they did things during the summer holidays on beautiful sunny days. Then, I could hear birds singing and bees humming. There would be flowers blooming but I would be going through hell as everyone else walked around in shorts, eating ice cream and talking about what a lovely day it was. On cold, dark nights when everything was more barren, it almost seemed more acceptable that dark, terrible things were happening.

Hallowe'en, Easter, Christmas – they would use all the props. Each event was a learning experience – I learned how they wanted me to act and react, but I was also learning another thing – I was getting close to my breaking point. I would get out of this one day.

CHAPTER 18

CHANGES

My heart is sore
I want no more

I hated my name. Although they didn't always call me by it, I still loathed the sound of 'Lorraine'. For me, it was associated with everyone I despised and everything I feared about my life.

I could never tell when I would be called 'Lorraine' or something else. Often, someone would shout, 'Gillian! Come and stand here.' None of us knew who they meant. There would be no 'Gillian'. So, someone would step forward – if it was decided they were the 'wrong' person, they would be punished. If they were the right person at that time, but went forward the next time the name was called, they might find they were not the right person anymore. There was no rhyme or reason to it.

There was no way to know. We never looked at each other; we didn't know the real names of each child. It was all guesswork; it was all messing with us.

They didn't even have consistent names for themselves. In the white house, they had tended to call each other 'brother' or 'sister', but when it all moved on to the bigger group, those terms weren't used. The most frequent word used was 'Daddy'. When that was applied to someone, it would be in a sleazy way. By this stage, they were taking photographs and filming the abuse, and I assume that they were conforming to quite clichéd paedophiliac fantasies. I don't think that I really noticed when the photographing or filming of the abuse began. That isn't surprising really. When you are being hurt as much as I was, you focus on getting through it rather than anything else.

However, I did start to become aware of situations which were almost like set pieces. Adults, usually but not always men, would be sitting in chairs with masks on, when I was taken in to be abused. Quite often, they would already be masturbating when I arrived. Then they would hold their hand out and say, 'Come to Daddy,' when I walked in.

Invariably, someone would be filming this. It was all random to me, but everything would be planned by them. They knew what they were doing – perhaps they rehearsed, I think they probably must have done. I had no idea what was planned each time. All I knew was that I needed to keep some part of me separate.

I decided to change my name.

When I was nine, I chose to be called Laurie. They didn't know. No one from that time or that part of my life knew, but I promised myself that, when I got away, I would never answer to Lorraine again. I kept that promise and it has served me well. To this day, whenever someone calls me by my old name, I know they are from a time of my life that I would much rather forget. It's a way of slotting them into that time. Andrew had always used my name in a particular way, too, and I wanted to get away from that now that I saw the danger in what he had done. He always said it very softly, rolling it as he spoke, and dragging it out. It was very different to the way my mum sharply shouted it when she wanted to give me a row for something.

I was surrounded by control and planning, and yet I had no control over my own life. I have since wondered whether the time during which all of this took place was important. Britain had not long been out of the Second World War and the country was still recovering. Older people – people of the age of my abusers – still had memories of that in their minds, and their experiences had been shaped by what everyone had gone through. There is a strong possibility that the people who made my life a misery had actually learned some of what they practised from what was happening on a wider scale. The Nazi enemy had not only been adept at control and emphasising the fight between strength and weakness, but they had also been masters at whipping crowds up into orgasmic frenzies.

I don't know whether there was a direct political element to what some of these people practised, but they definitely had parallels with some of the cultural and global activities which we were only now hearing about. There was an element of racism in their activities, too. Lots of people were casually racist in those days, but my abusers would frequently disparage the colour of my skin. If you met me now, you wouldn't think twice about my colouring – perhaps I'm not quite as pale as a lot of Scottish people, but I certainly don't look 'foreign'. And yet that is exactly what was levelled at me. Did they know about my dad's blood line? Or were they so strongly pro-white that any suggestion of mixed-race irritated them?

They would always find something they could pick on. They would use my left-handedness to suggest that I was the spawn of the Devil, and they would say I had dirty skin. They said that my darkness was a mark of my allegiance with the dark itself, but that didn't make sense because they themselves were supposedly in league with the 'dark side'.

I resolved myself not to care. I'd make resolutions every night in bed, resolutions not to care, not to let them get to me. 'I don't care about anything,' I'd tell myself. 'I don't care about animals; I don't care about loving anyone.'

But I did. I always loved animals. However, I did manage to learn not to care about people. I became very thick-skinned.

Much to my shame, I started to wish that they would choose other children when the abuse began. That's a horrible place to get to, but I did. They would sometimes ask me to choose a child and before I had hated that and struggled with it. Now, I didn't care. There were never real choices anyway. When they asked me to choose someone to be abused, they had already made their choice, and they would take that child while telling me I had done the wrong thing again. I always did.

I watched all of the time for a sign of which way to jump.

That is one skill I have kept with me – I'm very good at interpreting body language, although the situations in which I do so now are thankfully very much different. I tried to second guess them all of the time, but it never mattered. They had things planned regardless of what I, or anyone else, said. I don't think I necessarily realised that at the time because they sometimes gave us the illusion of power. When you are completely powerless and someone says, 'You choose,' you have an illusion that you can make things different. You wonder whether things will change if only you get the right answer. All you have to do is choose. They have put the ball in your court, and all you have to do is get it right. It'll never happen, but it takes a long time for that flicker of hope to disappear.

Did I ever get anything right? Only when I followed instructions to the letter. Getting it right and getting praise only happened when I was a complete slave to what they wanted. When I fought that little girl and smashed her head with the stone, I got a lot of praise and was told I was finally doing something right. They liked when I didn't cry. Crying always made them shout about signs of weakness. They expected instant collusion, and we all learned that was what we had to do.

How much was sexual and how much was physical? The physical and emotional violence was, for me personally, worse than the sexual abuse, and it happened every time. The sexual violence, in my eyes, was just part of how the world was. The only time it varied was when the physical abuse came into it, too.

So, I was raped, and that was my life. Andrew had made it so that I didn't know the difference between what was normal for children and what was not. When I had visited Fiona's house and saw that she was exposed to it, too, then that had reinforced to me that abuse was just how the world worked. Within the context of what was done to me, I thought rape was ordinary.

Even at that point, at nine, I was still harbouring the illusion that what happened with Andrew was fine. I actually thought it was all right in certain circumstances for a child to be raped. When emotional and psychological factors were brought into it all, though, I was thrown. It impacted on me hugely. For example, the way I relate to food was moulded by those years and is still a factor in my adult life, whereas I have a loving relationship with my partner, which has transcended what was done to me sexually. So, which was worse? No one should have to choose.

This is exactly the type of struggle so many survivors face every day. I still can't touch some of the foods I was tormented with. I try to cook them for my children, but even when I've made them from scratch, I still can't eat them. I have tried to reclaim them, but I just can't eat things like rice. The texture takes me back to that time. I think it is the association with vomiting that is the problem, and the memory of being made to eat it again. I know that some people will find it odd that these are the lingering problems, rather than ones related to the sexual abuse, but I'll bet there are an awful lot of people who are reading this and thinking, 'I thought it was only me ...' There are no rules as to what may be a trigger for a survivor, and I have had many surprises over the years.

Things were changing, I was changing, but there were also sometimes links with previous events that I couldn't make sense of. Years earlier, Andrew had sent me on a 'message' to a house in our local area. Nothing had happened. The two men there hadn't touched me. I think it had just been a test to see how compliant I was. However, one or the other of them started to meet me at school.

When the first man was waiting for me after school one day, I was slightly confused. I didn't often see the same person twice, but I knew this one hadn't been in my life for a long time. He opened the car door and I got in.

As always, I lay on the floor. We hadn't driven for long when he parked. He opened the door and dragged me out by my arm. It was the same house I had gone to that time long ago.

He shoved me roughly inside and locked the front door. The house was filthy and smelled like the old sofa I had previously been attacked on. 'Get through there,' he barked, and indicated a door which was slightly ajar.

When I went in, the other man was lying on the bed with his trousers and pants off. He got up and came over to me. He had obviously been masturbating, but at the sight of me he got excited again.

They tied me up that day. They used ropes and they tied me to the bed frame. They touched me, but didn't rape me. What I soon realised was that, for them, it was the school

189

uniform that was the attraction. Within their clichéd, dangerous fantasy, they were both attracted to that symbol of a child's innocence. Every time one of them collected me, it would always be from school and I would always be in uniform. It was all very much about having use of a small schoolgirl. Sometimes they tied me to a chair, sometimes to a bed, sometimes to an electrical flex – the only thing that stayed the same was my uniform.

They went to great pains to ensure that, when they masturbated, they never got anything on my clothes. I wonder if this was because they thought that, while a child might not recognise things, a parent might (and some of the children may have had more attentive parents – we'll never know). They only ever masturbated themselves; they never asked me to do it for them. Sometimes they did it to each other. I felt like a doll, a prop.

For me, it was almost a side issue. It was extra abuse. It completely reinforced what was going on elsewhere as it just told me, yet again, that I was there for anyone to use however they pleased. I was just an object. Those guys would reappear in different contexts – sometimes they would be at the farmyards or deserted schoolrooms, too. It was as if they were recycling me. I have wondered whether they had come to a separate arrangement with Andrew to use me outside of those places. Had they gone freelance? Was my uncle sub-contracting me? Or had they thought of it themselves?

Sometimes, while I was in their house being abused, I could hear children outside playing. They were doing perverted things to a schoolchild, while the world went on as always. I would listen to the children outside, and it was a world in which I didn't belong. That was the worst bit. The street where the house was located was a busy one. There were always lots of children around. Perhaps these men were fathers themselves; for all I know, their own children could have been playing outside while they defiled me. The house they used seemed neglected. It was probably abandoned, but the area in general was always hectic.

They didn't use the language or torture of the group abuse. They didn't talk about weakness and strength. For them, it was simply the clichéd paedophiliac fantasies of me being a good little girl and them being the Daddies. I don't know how long it went on, but I don't remember them abusing me when I was at high school. It was about having access to a young schoolgirl. Sometimes they would spank me, but they weren't particularly physically violent, not in relation to what I was used to. However, they did make me very uncomfortable. It slotted into the normalisation of things for me, but the setting bothered me. I had thought, for so long, that every child was raped and abused, but the noises of the happy children outside wouldn't leave my head. They haunted me. Was that sort of happiness something that other children enjoyed regularly? I wondered whether they were happy despite leading a life like mine or whether – and this was a new thought for me – they had happy lives, lives free from abuse. Normal lives.

I was starting to think about what else there might be. Laurie was starting to question what Lorraine never had.

CHAPTER 19

SNAPPED

Please let me die
Don't make me lie anymore.
Because I'm bad
They make me sad.

When I was about nine, something inside me snapped. I stopped being so quiet and accepting in the 'normal' world. I had been a teacher's gift up until that point. I was certainly strange but they must have loved me in terms of my academic behaviour. I caused no trouble. If they had said 'Jump', I'd have asked, 'How high?'

The most challenging thing I ever did up until then was steal food from the school dinners, but I was clever about it and no one noticed so I hadn't been labelled a problem child. Perhaps I should have got myself noticed, after all. Perhaps if I had been labelled a problem child, someone would have asked questions and dug a little deeper.

At nine, I reached a place where something broke inside me and I just couldn't cope with it anymore. It was initially in school that these feelings manifested themselves. I don't know what it was – probably a combination of feeling like an alien, hating who I was, hating the world, hating adults, being terrified of adults, being terrified of becoming one, being terrified of becoming one of the enemy. It was quite a list – there were so many problems, but I think it was the latter which was the main one in many ways, the one which pushed me into snapping. I didn't want to be someone who hurt kids but I thought that was what would happen. I thought it was inevitable. This is what happens when you grow up, I told myself, so I don't want to grow up.

I suspect that there was also the fact that the abuse was escalating. I was getting to an age where my body could cope with it. It was getting so frequent and so intense, and my only hope – that God could help me – had proved futile. I couldn't go on but I couldn't defy my parents or my family or my uncle. I had no choices there so what could I do?

Doing something at school was my only option.

One day, I went into my classroom and completely trashed it. I went ballistic. I broke everything I could get my hands on; I smashed it all up and, in the eyes of the teachers, it came out of nowhere. As I sat in the middle of the debris, one teacher, Mrs Anderson, gingerly came over to me while I caught my breath. I had demolished everything around me.

'Lorraine?' she said. 'Lorraine, what is it? What's wrong?'

Before I could answer her – and I have no idea whether I would have said anything anyway – another teacher came storming into the classroom.

'Lorraine Matthew! What on earth do you think you're doing?' she shouted. 'For goodness sake! Look at the damage; look at what you've done, girl!'

She ranted and raved, just as my mother would have done, and then she said what I had heard so many times, 'Your parents will be so disappointed. They're good people and they will be embarrassed and ashamed at what you have brought on your family! You're a disgrace, young lady, a disgrace!' She dragged me to the head teacher's office where I heard the same things again. Mrs Anderson didn't come with me and I heard no more kind words that day.

I don't know what I had expected to happen, but I was sent back to class once it had been cleaned up. No one could understand why I had done what I did, and no one really wanted to ask any questions which might get to the bottom of it. I felt a burning rage inside me, and I wanted to keep going, to grab their attention, to show them I had the power to scream 'LOOK! LOOK AT ME! LOOK AT THE HORROR I'M LIVING!' I was crying out for help, but no one heard me. No one was listening.

That day was such a momentous one for me, though. From always trying to be hidden, I was suddenly making myself visible. At lunchtime, I felt as if every child in the whole school was watching me. I stood alone – Fiona and I hadn't really had much to do with each other since the time I had stayed over at her house – but I could feel their eyes on me. I did nothing, but it felt as if everything was intensified. I could hear everyone else, I could hear their words and their noise so clearly, but I felt completely detached. There was a group of kids who were the resident bullies. They didn't really bother with me, because I had a reputation for being strange, but they picked on little kids. I hated that. I hated bullies victimising weaker children. They were doing it that day, just as they did every day, but I couldn't stand by and watch it any longer.

I slowly walked over to a group of them. They were standing, laughing at some poor girl who they had just been ridiculing – and I launched into them. I was hitting, punching, kicking, scratching. Nothing could stop me. I had gone from being the quietest child in the school to a vigilante. I was in such a rage that day. The same thing happened again and a teacher came out and dragged me back to the head teacher, but nothing changed.

Around this time, my brother came out of hospital. I didn't really know him, but I had a powerful instinct to protect him. I had no idea whether he would be in danger from Andrew or anyone else, but I wasn't willing to take the chance. I wanted to protect him better than I had protected myself.

I think that the combination of all of these things made me realise that, ironically, you did have to be strong. No one would come to save you, no one was coming to be your saviour. 'Be strong' were the words that my abusers used and they were right. Those were the exact messages I had been given and that was how it was. The things that they had told me to keep me abused were the things that I needed to survive being abused and which would get me out of being abused. There was no way I could have consciously thought that out but it was the reality of my life. It was like *1984*. I was living in two different worlds.

I started trying to get some space where I could be alone. I began going out during the night, because if I went out when it was dark, no one could get me. I lived in a tenement three storeys up but I would climb out of the window and down a drainpipe. Looking back, that was pretty dangerous, but night-time in my bedroom was more dangerous, it was the worst place I could possibly be.

I was always anxious when I was in bed at night. Even if nothing happened, it was awful. If nothing happened I'd just be sitting there, dripping in sweat, waiting for someone to come and it all to start again. Basically, I was going out into the street and doing crazy things to get some control over my own life. I remember one night taking everyone's washing off the washing lines in their back gardens. I jumped it all in puddles of mud and hung it back up again. It took ages and made no sense but it was something I chose to do, no one else forced me into it and that was important.

A few days after I had smashed up the schoolroom and attacked the bullies, Mrs Anderson took me aside and asked me what was wrong. I just shrugged and shook my head. 'Is there anything you want to tell me, Lorraine?' she asked. I shook my head again. 'I've noticed something – but I don't know what it is. You tell me.'

I couldn't.

I've always remembered that moment – someone *had* noticed something. But nothing came of it.

Changing my name was vitally important. It was something I did by myself, for myself. The others never knew Laurie. I didn't tell anyone to start with, but when the shift happened in me, the notion to do this was in my head. It was my secret. My parents never knew; no one could ever know – that way they would never penetrate the real me. I didn't care what name they used – that person wasn't me. They could call me Lorraine but I was able to dissociate myself and keep a part of me away. My name had changed in my mind so now I had a secret 'Laurie' inside me. I needed there to be a piece of me they didn't have. I had to have something. It was so personal that no one knew, not even Andrew.

It was just what I needed. I was having huge difficulties with trying to fathom who I was. I hated what was happening and I felt that I had no identity apart from that of a child who was constantly abused. I wasn't seen as anything else. The time between the ages of four and ten is hard to draw out; where does one thing end and another start?

The flickering flame of questioning in me made everything harder. If I had accepted it all, then things would have been easier. I loved education, I was clever, I desperately wanted to be a doctor or a vet, but there was no way I was going to follow either of those options unless I accepted the niggle inside me that what was happening was wrong. I didn't like what was happening but I made it harder by questioning it.

Snapped

I was learning one thing by now and one thing alone – it wasn't right. I wasn't the one who was wrong and who acted in a way different to the rest of the world. They were wrong, these people who were hurting me and I wanted it to stop. I desperately wanted it to stop.

'I'll never forget this,' I said to myself, one night as I lay on the floor of a car being driven back. 'I'll never forget. Never.'

CHAPTER 20

IT CAN'T BE TRUE, CAN IT?

I think I'm dead.
I hate my bed.
Please set me free.
Please let me be.

The people who were behind my abuse were very clever. They had created something which would be so difficult to explain, so difficult to make sense of, that it would be easier to dismiss it all out of hand as the ramblings of an over-imaginative child.

Many people don't want to believe that child abuse exists, or are only willing to believe that certain kinds of abuse go on. They don't want to consider that something so horrific, and yet so widespread, is taking place in their community, perhaps only a door away from them, a few steps from their lives – or even in their lives if they would only open their eyes.

I know this, not just because of my own personal experience, but through my work supporting and listening to survivors and those still experiencing abuse.

To ask people not only to believe in the abuse but also to take on board all the details of what I'm revealing is a big step, and it has taken me many years to make the decision to tell my story, but it has to be done. This type of abuse is ongoing, as is the culture of disbelief to make people dismiss anyone who talks about it. This needs to be challenged. The things I'm telling you in this book have been kept close to me all of my life; I have always known that talking of them, telling the full story, would make some people incredulous – but it's true. It's all true.

Whatever the set dressing, they were rapists and abusers – plain and simple. The trappings that surrounded the abuse was just a way of creating something that would allow them to do what they wanted to, but which would also allow for confusion on our parts, and devotion on the parts of the 'followers'. I think this is what many people find so hard when they are asked to believe in this sort of abuse. It all seems so fantastical, so it's easy to dismiss. I'm not asking you to believe in any of that. I'm not asking you to believe in Satan, I'm not even asking you to believe in God. I'm just asking you to accept that there are some people who will go to extraordinary lengths to cover up the fact that they are abusing children.

What words are there to describe what happened to me; what was done to me? Some call it ritual abuse, others call it organised abuse. There are those who call it satanic. I've heard all of the phrases, not just in relation to me, but also with regard to those I work with and try to help. Do you know what I think? It doesn't matter how you dress it up, it doesn't matter what label you put on it. It is abuse, pure and simple. It is adults abusing children. It is adults deciding – actually making a conscious decision, a conscious choice – that what they want, what they convince themselves they need, is more important than anything else; certainly more important than the safety or feelings or sanity of a child.

However, there can be differences which are layered on top of that abuse. I'm not saying that some abuse is worse than others, or that someone 'wins' the competition to have the worst abuse inflicted on them, but ritual and organised abuse is at the extreme end of the spectrum. If we try to think of a continuum where there are lots of different things imposed on children (or, for that matter, anyone who is forced into these things – and that force can take many forms, it can be threats and promises, as well as kicks and punches), then ritual and organised abuse is intense and complicated.

It often involves multiple abusers of both sexes. There can be extreme violence, mind control, systematic torture and even, in some cases, a complex belief system which is sometimes described as religion. I say 'described as' religion because, to me, I think that when this aspect is involved, it is window dressing. I'm not religious. I cried many times for God to save me. I was always ignored – how could I believe? However, I think that ritual abusers who do use religious imagery or 'beliefs' are doing so to justify it all to themselves, or to confuse the victim, or to hide their activities.

Ritual abuse is highly organised and, obviously, secretive. It is often linked with other major crimes such as child pornography, child prostitution, the drugs industry, trafficking, and many other illegal and heinous activities. Ritual abuse is organised sexual, physical and psychological abuse, which can be systematic and sustained over a long period of time. It involves the use of rituals – things which the abusers 'need' to do, or 'need' to have in place – but it doesn't have to have a belief system. There doesn't have to be God or the Devil, or any other deity for it to be considered 'ritual'. It involves using patterns of learning and development to keep the abuse going and to make sure the child stays quiet.

There has been, and still is, a great deal of debate about whether or not such abuse actually exists anywhere in the world. There are many people who constantly deny that there is even such a thing as ritual abuse. All I can say is that I know there is. Not only have I been a victim of it myself, but I have been dealing with survivors of this type of abuse for almost 30 years.

If there are survivors, there must be something that they have survived.

The thing is, most sexual abuse of children is ritualised in some way. Abusers use repetition, routine and ritual to force children into the patterns of behaviour they require. Some abusers want their victims to wear certain clothing, to say certain things. They might bathe them or cut them, they might burn them or abuse them only on certain days of the week. They might do a hundred other things which are ritualistic, but aren't always called that – partly, I think, because we have a terror of the word and of accepting just how premeditated abuse actually is.

Abusers instil fear in their victims and ensure silence; they do all they can to avoid being caught. Sexual abuse of a child is rarely a random act. It involves thorough planning and preparation beforehand. They threaten the children with death, with being taken into care, with no one believing them, with physical violence or their favourite teddy being taken away. They are told that their mum will die, or their dad will hate them, the abusers say everyone will think it's their fault, that everyone already knows they are bad. Nothing is too big or too small for an abuser to use as leverage.

There is unmistakable proof that abusers do get together in order to share children, abuse more children, and even learn from each other. As more cases have come into the public eye in recent years, this has become increasingly obvious. More and more of this type of abuse is coming to light.

I definitely think that it is the word ritual which causes most people to question, to feel uncomfortable, or even just to disbelieve. It seems almost incredible that such things would happen, but too many of us know exactly how bad the lives of many children are. A great deal of child pornography shows children being abused in a ritualised setting, and many have now come forward to share their experiences, but still there is a tendency to say it just couldn't happen.

Why not?

Why, given what we now know about paedophiles and about what they do to children? Would they have limits? It was all done to me and I have enough experiences to write many more books than this one, but this will have to do for now. I've tried to make sense of it and I've tried to tell you my story in a way that will, hopefully, let you understand how it was done, and how they managed to get away with it, but I haven't told you a big part of it yet. I haven't told you what happened that finally ended it all for me.

There was something else.

When I was eight, someone else came into my life and made a huge difference to what was happening and how things would turn out. I didn't know it then, but I see the whole picture now.

Something I have often wondered is whether Andrew was there while I was being abused. Lots of people hid their faces, and there were often masks worn, so he certainly could have been. I have no evidence one way or another though, so will leave it to the reader to decide whether it would seem in a paedophile's character to watch abuse continue when it had been masterminded by him. But I do know that it wasn't just me who he abused – I know that because I saw it.

Andrew was away a lot with the Army until I was at high school, then he left that position. He was instrumental both in my abuse and in setting the scene, but when I was eight, something happened which would distract him and which would, at times, take his attention from me. My mother very kindly provided him with a new victim – my little sister.

When my baby sister was born, the contrast couldn't have been greater. Sharron was everything I wasn't. She soon turned into a pretty little girl who wasn't greedy and who was thin and petite. I was the fat one, supposedly, who would stuff her face with food whenever she got a chance, knowing that my mother might not remember to feed me for a while again.

The only thing I had which Sharron hadn't, was that I was clever; but even that got turned against me. All I heard from people was that I was 'too clever for my own good'. I never did understand that. How could you be too clever? If you were extra clever, how could that be a bad thing? Sharron wasn't clever; she never did embrace education or want to learn everything she could about as many things as possible, and this was seen as a positive part of her personality. Not only was I too clever, I was arrogant and I was sullen, according to my family. Really, I had nothing going for me – but no one ever stopped to ask why.

There was a natural split between us when Sharron was born because I was eight years older. Obviously, I wasn't a child who knew anything of love or normal relationships, so there was no excitement about a baby coming into my world. For many little girls and boys, the anticipation of a new brother or sister can feel wonderful. They prepare for it, buy the new sibling a gift, get told how they will be able to help out and how they will be so grown up with all of the things they will be able to do – there was none of that for me. I had no interest in other children or babies, and there was no happy family dynamic which helped me into my new role.

Mum was pregnant, then there was Sharron.

That was it.

I hated her with a vengeance. She was a little angel who was wanted by my mother and who was pretty. Sharron was a wonderful little girl to everyone. I don't think my mother ever lifted a hand to her, and I think Sharron would confirm that.

My main reason for hating her, though, was an awful one. I was scared that she would take Andrew from me. And as she grew, his attention did begin to shift to her. I would love to say that I was only looking to protect my little sister but the truth was I was jealous. He began to change from being my special person to not really being that interested in me at all. And, all the while, my abuse elsewhere continued. His love, his special attention had been all that kept me going, and now it was disappearing.

I wanted to keep him away from her – but for the wrong reasons. In my head he was mine, he was my special person but, of course, as I was getting older, his interest in me was waning anyway.

I don't know whether it was because he had lost interest in me, or because the abuse elsewhere was so horrific, particularly without him in my life to make things seem better but, whatever the reason, I soon moved from wanting him to leave Sharron alone for my sake, to wanting him to leave her alone for the right reasons. She was tiny, just a toddler, and the thought of him touching her or abusing her horrified me. I started trying to attract his attention whenever he looked at her. I'd dance, I'd sing, I'd sit on his lap. I'd do a hundred things which were completely out of character – anything, anything to avoid seeing that look in his eye when he glanced at the baby.

I knew that he was planning to do to her what he had done to me. I tried to get in the way, I tried to get him to play with me, but once Sharron was about three, the penny finally dropped. I had always thought that he wasn't in the same category as the others; they weren't nice, and he always was. But as she began to replace me, it made me face up to things. What Uncle Andrew did wasn't right.

I was still acting up at school and I was always ready to fight for others. One day, I smashed all of the windows in class because the teacher refused to let even a breath of fresh air in for a girl who felt sick. I was setting fires in the local community. It was all becoming too much.

And now, now I had someone else to look after.

I was still having to sleep and eat and be dependent on home, but the other life was breaking into my every thought. I ran away dozens of times and I was still getting beaten by my mother on my return. I was still an outcast – it was becoming intolerable.

Even though I loved my uncle and craved his attention, the thought of him coming into my bed was starting to repulse me. Sharron slept in my bed, too, by then, and I wanted that to continue because I wanted to protect her.

Of course, there were plenty of times when I wasn't there. I was still being taken away to be abused, I was at school; and Sharron was often left unprotected. Something must have been happening because she started wetting the bed almost every night. This was a sign that even I couldn't turn away from. Sharron was being abused. I was sure of it. But I wouldn't stand for it, not for much longer.

CHAPTER 21

BREAKING

I won't cry; I want to die.
My heart is cold and I am old and all alone.
I am a stone.

It had to come to a head. Things simply couldn't keep going the way they were. One night, when I was about eleven and Sharron was three, it happened.

I was lying there while she slept and I was on alert. I was listening for Andrew – and I heard him. He walked into the dark room and stood at the foot of our bed. He was just standing there, waiting. As if he was making up his mind. When he finally began to walk over to the bed, I sat up. 'Uncle Andrew?' I said. 'What are you doing?' I never usually asked anything, so this was out of character.

'Nothing. Nothing,' he replied. It was a lie. He came closer to me and got in the bed at my side. He put his arms around me and started to touch underneath my night-clothes. The details don't matter. He did what he had done so many times in the past.

After it was over, after he had raped me, he got off me and walked round to the other side of the bed. He was going the wrong way. He needed to go to the door. I'd done what he wanted – so why was he going to her? Why was he going to my little sister? In my heart, I knew the answer. I'd watched for months now as he groomed her just as he'd groomed me. The way he played with her. The way he gave her presents. The way he touched her. And now? Now he was going to rape her.

Much as I loved him, he should not be there. It was wrong. Sharron started to whimper, then she began to cry, but he wouldn't stop. She was crying for Mum, and she was horribly upset. I'm not her, this is her story and I have no right to go into the details of it, but when he was done, he simply walked away.

'I want Mummy!' wept Sharron.

I tried to stop her going through. I still knew better than to tell, but she was sobbing. She had wet the bed and was obviously in physical pain. I couldn't prevent her.

She ran through to my parents' room and I listened at the door. I don't know what Sharron said but I did hear my mum. I can still hear her words in my head as if they were yesterday.

'He didn't mean it.'

'It was an accident.'

'Put some cream on yourself.'

I could hear Sharron continue to sob. I was horrified by Mum's response, but I also thought, you're not meant to tell, we'll be in such trouble.

Breaking

I went back to our room and changed the bed. A few minutes later, Sharron came through in one of Dad's shirts with cream on her where she had been abused. What did that say to me – and to her? That everything 'they' said was right and everything I thought was wrong; it was still me who was the alien.

I hadn't been able to save Sharron.

What I didn't know, however, was that Andrew had made a terrible mistake. Not a moral one, not a practical one, but one of evidence. I had seen him. I was a witness. Sharron may have been too small to say anything or understand anything about what he had done to me so many times in front of her, but this was different. He had slipped up. It might take over 40 years before he paid for it, but he would.

Things were happening for me, too. I was getting older and my body was changing. I was of less interest to Andrew as I turned into a woman, but my own development would be the next stage of my move towards breaking away.

I didn't know what to think about anything, that hadn't changed. Was it right to tell myself that I'd never forget? I've often thought of this as the years have gone by. As someone who now helps those who have gone through sexual abuse, or who are still experiencing it, I have seen many ways of coping. No one approach is absolutely right, no one approach is absolutely wrong, but there are some people who need to put what has been done to them in the past. I always said that I would never forget and I wonder whether my life would have been different had I not made that vow to myself. If I had locked it all away, would I be doing what I do now? I know that what I endured has made me the woman I am today, and I feel that I am privileged to have met so many wonderful, strong, resilient individuals; but if I had been the sort of person who decided to put it away in a little box when I finally escaped, would I have taken another path in life?

Saying that I would 'never forget' in no way means that I have spent every day of my life thinking about what happened. I think about it when I have to, when it will help someone else if I can remember, or when I just can't keep it out. Writing this book has been hard, perhaps harder than I imagined when I started the process, as I have, inevitably, remembered even more details of those terrible times.

Things stay with me. I'd never had a choice – not when my mother emotionally and physically abused me, not when my Uncle Andrew began grooming me, not when any of the dozens of sick individuals stole my childhood from me over the years and put their needs and wants first.

As I continued to try to run away, I soon became known to the police. I would regularly be caught trying to hitch a lift out of Dundee. Drivers would often report me and the police would pick me up and take me home. The irony is that the drivers who went to the police were probably concerned for my safety. They had no idea what it was they were sending me back to. My geography didn't help matters. The first time I tried to get to London, I stood on the wrong side of the dual carriageway. When a lorry stopped,

I asked the driver to take me as far as he was going and promptly fell asleep. When I woke up, we were in Inverness – completely the wrong direction – and it had the same outcome. The police were called for the poor lost girl wandering around the service station and I was taken back to the very place which was worst for me.

The script hadn't changed since the first time I had tried to get away when I was seven. The police would give me a lecture about what a terrible worry I was to my family, about how I put them through so much, about what a bad child I was for tormenting them. Mum would rant and rave, and generally put on a great impression of a concerned parent, before knocking me from one side of the room to the other as soon as they left.

It's still happening. There are thousands of others like me out there as you read this. There are thousands of children who will finally, somehow, manage to get away, only to be dragged back to the centre of the abuse by the police and people 'helping' them. Nothing has changed.

So much of my life I had no control over, but there was one thing that even my abusers couldn't control. They couldn't stop Nature.

Puberty would save me. On the day that I got my first period, I ran. It hit me that this changed everything. I wouldn't – I couldn't – get pregnant by any of them. The thought of bringing a baby into this was even worse than anything I had previously imagined.

So, when I was fourteen, the running away finally worked. I finally escaped.

CHAPTER 22

LONDON

I have to find a place to hide
An island in the sea
Surrounded by a racing tide
Where I can live with me

I was walking under a big black cloud at fourteen. I thought the whole world was out to get me and that safety was nowhere. I was probably suffering from depression, but I also had no idea what normal was. Everyone thinks that once you are free from the abuse, everything is fine. It's not. You have memories and flashbacks; it can take years to recover − if you ever do. I trusted no one, and my only thought was for survival.

When I made the decision to leave that final time, in 1968, I knew only that I needed to get to London, and there was only one thing I had to take with me. A few years earlier I had acquired a dog, Sheltie, who was the centre of my world.

I had got Sheltie from the dog pound just before he was to

be put to sleep for biting people. He had actually been very badly treated and was a lovely dog when treated with love and respect. I was allowed to keep him because Mum saw him as a status dog – he was the most beautiful rough-coated collie and would have cost a fortune originally. Mum saw him as a step up from the usual strays I wanted. She thought more of the reaction of the neighbours, who would think we were well-off to have such a beautiful pure-bred creature than the fact that I wanted him so much. I adored Sheltie, as I had always adored all animals, but had forever been terrified that 'they' would get him. That I had kept him safe was the one small comfort in my life, and I truly didn't think I could cope without him. So, I took Sheltie and I ran. I hitchhiked all the way to London and ended up in the city centre. The first place I can remember was Piccadilly Circus. The noise and the bustle was incredible and that suited me fine. It was the place to be to get lost, to disappear and to find yourself. To begin with, I only needed the lost part.

I knew someone in London. A girl called Rachel had lived a few doors away from me in Dundee. She was about a year older and had been put in a home due to the fact that she was 'seeing' a 40-year-old bus driver called Stevie. Rachel had run away, too. She and Stevie were now living in a flat with his daughter who was my age.

I had an address for Rachel and Stevie, and that was where I planned to go. I assumed that the police were look-ing for me, but I later found out that my parents hadn't bothered to report me missing. I thought I was on the run, but no one cared. I kept moving, thinking that I was the subject of a massive search, but there was no one desperately seeking a lost fourteen-year-old called 'Lorraine'. There were too many of us, really. So, I landed at Rachel's flat and tried to work out what to do. However, it did not work out living with the two of them.

What I hadn't expected was the difficulty in having Sheltie with me. I could cope – just about – with being cold and hungry, but I couldn't face him being the same way. Not long after I left for London, I had to go back to Dundee to take Sheltie home, hoping he would be looked after better than I had ever been. I hitched all the way back, let myself into the house in the middle of the night, had a tearful farewell with my dog in silence, and then left again.

The journey back was harder than the first time. Not only was I without Sheltie, but I also had problems with the people who picked me up. When you hitch, you tend only to get a little way at a time, so the trip from Dundee to London took a long time and consisted of a lot of different vehicles. I suppose it's only to be expected that not all of them would be good people. One of the lorry drivers pulled off the motorway at one point and tried to rape me. I fought him off, jumped out of the cab in the pitch dark and screamed. He followed me, apologising all the time.

'I'm sorry!' he shouted. 'I thought you were up for it!'

I was fourteen and hitching. I guess he assumed it was a fair trade.

'Get back in,' he said. 'I really am sorry. We're in the middle of nowhere – I made a mistake. I'm so sorry, really I am.'

I was torn. I didn't trust anyone, but he was right – we

were in the middle of nowhere and I had just as much chance of being attacked by the next person who gave me a lift. At least this one knew that I wasn't 'up for it' and he was apologising.

'Come on – I'll drop you at the next service station,' he pleaded.

I got back in and he drove in silence.

After a few minutes, he pulled over into another lay-by, got out, walked round to my side and dragged me out.

'Fuck off,' he said as he walked back to his cab. 'Teasing fucking bitch.'

It was pitch black and I had no choice but to wander along the hard shoulder. I was finally reported by someone and picked up by the police. I told them that I was seventeen and was also extremely rude to the officer who kept asking me questions.

He seemed a kind man, but, as I've said so many times, I trusted no one.

'What's your name?' he asked, as I lied. 'Is there anything I can do for you?'

He kept at me, asking me things, trying to get my story and I just gave him a mouthful of abuse. That man actually restored my faith in people a little that night, though he never knew it and perhaps I didn't either at the time. He bought me cups of tea and sandwiches as we drove on, and when we finally got to the station, he made it clear that he would do all he could to help me, if only I would give him the chance.

In the morning, he was there again. He had to let me go.

'Listen,' he said as I got ready to leave, 'I've got daugh-ters – I can help.'

I scoffed at him.

'Really, I can – just let me.'

He could see that I was a kid with problems and he was a good man, but I didn't know how to react to kindness so I walked away. Why would he care? I thought. What was he after? I was worthless so he must have an agenda.

Trying to turn him into one of the bad guys, I pushed my cold hands into my pockets – and found a fiver. I knew that I had gone into that police station with nothing, and that he had put it there. A good man and no doubt a good father – I hope his kindness was repaid to him some day by someone.

Later, when I was healing, kind people like that came into my mind much more than the other type. On one occasion, a lorry driver who was giving me a lift stopped at a service station.

'Want something to eat?' he asked.

I shook my head, realising that he'd probably heard my rumbling stomach for the whole journey.

'You sure?' he pressed.

My rule of thumb was to take nothing. If I took nothing, I owed them nothing.

He looked at me and went inside. He came out a few minutes later with about half a dozen pre-packed sandwiches.

'I'm not that hungry,' he sighed. 'Take them – throw them away if you like. I don't know why I bought them in the first place.'

When he dropped me off, he said goodbye, then reminded me to take the food and dump it in a bin. His lights had barely faded before I was tucking into them ravenously.

I actually discovered, through trial and error, that truckers were safer on the whole than car drivers. The biggest problem they had was trying to stay awake and I didn't really want to talk. Although it was easier to get out of a car than a lorry if someone did attack me, it was a trucker's job at stake, so only a few of them tried anything. I hitched until I was nineteen, and I always looked for older truck drivers rather than the younger ones. Women drivers rarely stopped anyway. One night, a van screeched to a halt and the back doors opened. Two men jumped out and tried to drag me in. The reaction it provoked in me, taking me back to the other vans, meant they were dealing with a banshee. They had no chance. Escaping was new for me, but I never wanted to be in that position again.

Throughout the time I was in London, and all the hitching I did back and forward to check on Sharron, my head was exploding.

There isn't really anything you can do at fourteen to earn money legitimately. However, when you are that age and you've run away to London, being legitimate maybe isn't the first thing on your list of priorities. That isn't to say that there weren't things I refused to do because there were. I had never stolen before I ran away – apart from that one book – but I had to reassess that position. I needed to shoplift to stay alive. I had no clothes and no food – all I had were the things I had carried with me.

London

Finding food every day was so hard. If I'd gone into prostitution I'd have eaten. My mind was telling me to go for it, I'd been conditioned after all, but my heart said that if I went down that route, I'd never come back.

I started to think of myself as Laurie, the one who escaped, the one who got away. And if Laurie went back to allowing her body to be used, she would be Lorraine again. I didn't ever want to be Lorraine again.

Being in London at the end of the 1960s and early 1970s was an odd experience. I was alone and scared, but I'd also escaped. All around me people were talking about love and freedom. The song lyrics reflected what the rest of society was feeling – 'Flowers In Your Hair', 'Hitching a Ride' (ironically), 'San Francisco'. The Beatles were everywhere and I heard songs like 'All You Need Is Love' a hundred times a day, pouring out of cafes and shops. Music was changing. It was for young people and it signalled a new way of thinking which came from young people, too. The messages were about staying free, about hippies and flower power. It was a world away from my mum and dad dancing and singing to Jim Reeves or Bing Crosby.

I could hear this music from radios wherever I went and it gave me an insight into other people's lives. I could also pick up on news bulletins and I was aware, in snippets, of the war in Vietnam. A huge change was happening in the world and the only way I could think about my part in it was by writing poems, as I'd always done. I was drawn to the anti-war movement, to speeches about rights and freedom – I knew all about unfairness.

I started to wonder whether I could be part of something bigger and began to wonder about moving abroad. I settled on South Africa and was shocked when I found out that I needed a passport and some ID. I was in the process of trying to manoeuvre my way through the system when I hitched one night with a guy with a funny accent. It turned out that he was South African. The appalling racism and bigotry I listened to on that journey made me realise I could never go there. He told me that blacks were lazy, that they weren't real people, that they didn't feel or think in the same way as whites, and he also told me that – thankfully, in his opinion – there were plenty more people of the same opinion as him 'back home'. I felt unclean when I got out of that car.

I did go back to Dundee every so often, but never to see my parents. I only went to check up on Sharron. I had got away to London, but I hadn't escaped my own head. When you are in the middle of an abusive situation, you're in survival mode. You are just trying to stay alive. When you get out of that situation and know that you are alive, and that you are likely to stay alive, it changes how your head works. The energy which you put into survival now works against you. You start to think. You remember what you went through. It all floods into your brain because there is the opportunity for it to do so, perhaps the first opportunity ever.

During those five years on the streets of London, I would stay for a little while then find myself unable to cope. I'd go back to Dundee, hang around Sharron's school, check she was still alive, then leave again. This would be the pattern. There were no mobile phones, there were no Internet cafes. The only safe way I had to see how she was – superficially – was to go and look for myself. I knew she was still being abused (he wouldn't stop unless he was forced to stop), but I also knew from my own experiences that you could survive an awful lot. I just needed to make sure she was still breathing.

I slept in parks, in the underground and in railway stations. I had to stay alert to men, and occasionally women, trying to attack me, in order to steal anything I had, or trying to touch or abuse me. For a while, I moved into a squat with a load of hippies, but that lifestyle wasn't for me. They did a lot of drugs and believed in 'free love' so I moved on. I was like a piece of driftwood during that period; I never stayed anywhere for very long. One of the main reasons for this was because, once I got away from the abuse, I had flashbacks and panic attacks, and I found myself unable to trust anyone. My generally messed-up head made things unbearable. I couldn't settle anywhere. Running became what I did. I was so scared of everyone and, if anyone tried to get close, I ran. It was all I knew how to do now.

To stay alive on the streets, I stole. I picked people's pockets, I sneaked into houses and stole food. I also worked out where there was wastage – and there is so, so much of it. I took food from fruit stalls when they were closing and throwing out the old stuff, I was there when restaurants closed for the night. I started to work out what there was and how I could get it.

CHAPTER 23

LIVING

I have no hope. I have no choice.
And no one cares for me
I cannot fight. I have no voice.
Will running break me free?

I kept to myself, but you can't keep away from other people entirely when you live on the streets. As always, I tried to stay invisible, not to be noticed, but that was hard, too. I knew a few other girls and they couldn't understand why I wouldn't go on the game. One night a lass called Ann came up to me while I was settling down in a doorway in Piccadilly Circus.

'I'm starving,' she said. 'Are you?'

I nodded.

'Let's get a punter to buy us something, then,' she smiled.

We went to a nearby restaurant which she knew and a man did indeed buy us each a meal. Ann had told me that we just needed to say that we were going to the toilet, and then we could slip out the back door. We did – but he was waiting for us. He grabbed me but I managed to get away; and I never did that again.

I saw people as a risk. There were lots of squats at the time, and I would be invited to them on occasion, but I didn't see them as friends or the squats as safe places. I kept behind the scenes whenever I could, scavenging rather than begging. Everyone had their own areas and you could easily get a battering for going onto someone else's patch. On top of that, food issues were still there for me. To prove that I was in control – to myself – I wouldn't eat for a while, but then I would be in danger of collapsing and that would draw attention to me, so I had to be careful. I found my maintenance level.

There weren't always great pickings with regards to food anyway, but I was used to being hungry. There were chip shops and there was always food lying around near Theatreland. I slept in St James's Park and Hyde Park during summer, and often there would be picnic leftovers in the bins. I kept moving. I was young and vulnerable. If you are anywhere for more than three days, you get known and there's an assumption you're on the game, so I moved, moved, moved.

There were also a lot of drugs around as it was the time of 'turn on, tune in, drop out', but I didn't want to give up control so it all washed past me.

I was learning all the time, but there was always the worry about Sharron – where was she, who was she with, was she safe? I thought about her constantly, as well as having to look out for myself. There were so many rules that I learned. If you have a bag, it's assumed that you have something worth stealing, so a rucksack is the safest bet, as it's harder to steal. Try not to steal from shops as you are more likely to get noticed. Get clothes from washing lines instead. Sleep in public toilets. Back then you could sleep in the Underground, too, as there were no barriers to stop you going into certain places, and there were lots of nooks and crannies.

The main thing to remember was always to watch out for other people. At any point, you could be robbed and attacked, so you could never really rest or settle. It was actually safer to hitch and sleep, even if I didn't want to go anywhere.

The biggest problem was that I was young and I looked young. I was constantly approached by pimps. A girl on her own is unusual – they tend to belong to someone. I'd be offered free drugs to get me hooked so that I could be prostituted. I couldn't do that; I couldn't lose control.

There was a fair bit of violence against rough sleepers but I was not part of a group, not loud or noticeable, so it didn't really happen to me. London then, as now, was full of people wrapped up in themselves, happy to ignore what was under their noses until they were drunk or off their heads and looking for an easy target. There were CND marches and protests by hippies about everything, saying that they'd change the world – but they didn't want to change it for someone like me.

I felt as if I was screaming inside. I was desperate and had periods of feeling suicidal as I was so lonely and felt so dark. I liked and hated being invisible. Everything around me seemed so superficial. No one really thinks of the practicalities of the homeless. When I had my period, it was a nightmare – how could I get clean, get sanitary protection, rest if I was in pain?

Once I broke into a house on the outskirts of London. I was starving and took a risk. I saw an open kitchen window in the wee small hours and poured myself in. As I stood there, with my hand in the bread bin, the door opened and a woman walked in.

She looked terrified as I bolted back to the window, but as I made to climb up onto the worktop, I got the surprise of my life.

'Are you hungry?'

I looked round.

'Are you hungry?' she asked again.

I nodded.

'Come here, then,' she said, gently. 'I'll make you something.'

I was torn but my stomach won.

There didn't seem to be anyone else there, so I moved back in a little, but close enough to the window to get out if I had to.

'It's OK,' she kept saying, still gentle. 'It's OK. You have something to eat then you can be on your way. It's OK.'

She cooked some bacon and eggs for me. She urged me to sit down but I wouldn't. I couldn't risk that.

'Come here – you're hungry; I'll feed you.'

I watched her. I ate the food and left.

I thought she was after something but couldn't work out what. I remember her so well. She saw a hungry child and did the right thing. What a brave, kind lady she was.

There were a few people like that but the community in which I lived was not one to be romanticised. I saw what happened to other girls. They were quickly hooked on alcohol and drugs, made dependent and used for prostitution and pornography. But I didn't do those things. Laurie didn't do those things. You don't have to survive by losing yourself – and I did survive.

Finally, I knew that I couldn't rest knowing that my little sister was still there, in the middle of it, without me to provide what support I could.

I went back – but, this time, I knew I had to have it out with my mother.

I turned up, unannounced, at her door one day. Sharron was at school, Dad was at work, and I'd been watching the house long enough to know the house was empty apart from her. She looked shocked when she opened the door to me. She didn't look different at all, but I don't think she expected to see her hated daughter back.

'What do you want?' she snapped. There were no police officers to impress so she could be her real self.

'I want to talk to you,' I replied.

'Well, maybe I don't want to talk to you,' she said, bitterly. 'Running away like that. What a thing to do.' This was the odd thing about my mother. Although she'd never liked me, it was as if she was personally offended whenever I tried to run away. I would have thought she'd welcome any chance to be rid of me. It was all about the shame for her, though. She was only concerned about what the neighbours would think.

'Are you going to ask me in?' I queried.

She sighed. 'If I must.'

I squeezed in through the tiny bit of open space she had left me and walked into the living room. 'You know what I'm here for,' I said.

She shook her head, defiantly. 'I do not.'

'Yes. Yes you do, Mum. I need to talk to you about Sharron.'

'I don't want to talk about her. I don't want to talk about anything with you,' she replied.

I had to keep going. This wasn't about me, it was about my little sister, and I had to deal with my mum for her sake, not mine. 'I'm going nowhere,' I told her. 'I came here to talk to you about Sharron and that's exactly what I'm going to do. I don't care how long it takes. We will have this conversation, Mum.'

She stared at me and I could feel the same hatred which had been there for years. 'Hurry up, then,' she said finally. 'I've not got all day. What do you want?'

'It's simple. I want you to keep Andrew out of the house,' I told her.

'What? Why would I do that? What's that got to do with Sharron anyway?' she asked, a picture of innocence.

'You know exactly what it has to do with Sharron,' I replied. 'You keep him out of here; you keep him away from her.'

'Or what?' she snapped. 'What are you going to do?'

'I'll go to the police. I'll shout and scream and tell them everything.'

'You will not!' she hissed.

'I will. I promise you I will. All of the neighbours will know, Mum, everyone will know what this family lets happen, and they'll know exactly what you've allowed to go on under your nose in your house.'

'You wouldn't dare!' she said. She paused for a minute. 'Anyway – I don't know what you're talking about. I want you to leave now.'

I hadn't been invited to, but I sat down. I was shaking inside but I had to see this through for Sharron. I owed it to her.

'I dare, Mum,' I said. 'I dare. And you know very well what I'm talking about. I know. I know Sharron has told you.'

This was my trump card. I knew that Sharron had told lots of people that Andrew had abused her and that no one had ever believed her, but I also knew that when she had informed my mum of what our wonderful, upstanding uncle was capable of, she had responded, 'He's just missing his wife.'

She hadn't been shocked or appalled. She had justified it in five words.

'What do you want?' she asked again.

'I've told you. I want you to keep him away, or I'll go to the police.'

There was silence and I waited. I wasn't going to back

down on this and I would keep to my word if I had to. Finally, Mum said, 'Have it your way,' and stormed off into another room. I breathed a huge sigh of relief. If she meant it, if she did keep Andrew away, then I had done something.

I think she did keep to her word. As far as I know, he was kept from the house – but it didn't put my mind at rest in the way I had hoped. I realised that I would have to move back to Dundee for the foreseeable future to feel that I had any chance of helping Sharron. So, at nineteen, that is exactly what I did. I tried to settle but it was hard. I told myself that I knew who the bad guys were and, now I was older, they couldn't have the same control over me, but I hadn't accounted for how persistent they were or how my own demons were chasing me.

The other problem was that, although Andrew was being kept away from Sharron at my mum's house, his influence on her was still strong. She was eleven by now and could go to him if she chose to. The only option, it seemed, would be for her to move in with me. So that's what happened, but my little sister faced just the same terrors as I had. She was away from the abuse, but that allowed her the space to start thinking about the awful things that had been done to her.

Sharron couldn't cope. The problem is that, when you leave the abuse, it actually starts to fill your head. The flashbacks can be amazingly powerful and completely overwhelming. I watched Sharron go through this, just as I had done (just as I still did at times), and there wasn't anything I could do. She was safe while she was with me but her mind started processing everything that had been done to her. On top of that, Mum was angry that Sharron was with me and she was being very vocal about it. I was too big for her to hit now and in the past that had always been her main response. She was left without that option and, on top of that, she also had the fear that if she pushed me too far, I'd go to the police and rip her reputation to shreds in front of her neighbours and friends.

However, Sharron was old enough to make her own decisions and she chose to go back home. She'd lived with me for about six months and, during that time, I think she had met up with Andrew. The relationship between abuser and abused can be a complicated one. Andrew had a very strong hold on her, and would do for years to come. It is not my place to tell Sharron's story, she may very well choose to do that herself one day, but I do know that she was in a very different place from me.

I tried to settle without her, and I tried to tell myself that I had done all I could, but the guilt that I felt about Sharron was strong. I always felt I should have done more. I always will.

I was trying to make a life for myself, but my own past was trying to drag me back. When I finally got a place of my own, through the local authority, I received constant threats from my childhood abusers. In Dundee, among that group, there was obviously a fear that I might talk.

I thought I was seeing them everywhere. And I was.

They were there. They were all around. I started getting notes through my letterbox, making it quite clear that they knew where I lived and that they were watching me. They were never so silly as to threaten to kill me explicitly – they had always been cautious – but they did use the language they had always relied on to control me. I got a constant stream of letters saying that they could see me, talking about the all-seeing eye and the all-knowing nature of what I was part of. They threatened me for leaving, for trying to break away, and they made it very clear that they would never allow me any peace and that there was always someone 'keeping an eye' on me.

However, I had never said anything about what happened to me and I still felt no one would believe it. Sharron, on the other hand, had been telling everyone for years and no one believed her either. It didn't seem to matter which option we chose, it was useless.

Nobody listened.

One day I took a few things from my house and left. I disappeared for a while and, when I got back to Dundee, things seemed to have calmed down. I don't know why. I never did know how their minds worked. All I knew was that it was time for me to break free.

My own life was calling me.

CHAPTER 24

MAKING MY OWN DESTINY

I have no fear of other places
My fear is here in empty faces.
Fear makes me fast
Fear makes me strong
I'm running at last
Away from the wrong.

As time went by, I did settle more. When I was in my early twenties, I got a job at a garage and I was quickly made manager. I was never scared of hard work and the petty little things which can bog some people down never touched me. I had dealt with bigger worries than anything 'normal' life could throw at me.

What did bother me was that I had lost my chance to be what I wanted to be. I had never got the education I wanted and I felt that my opportunities there had been denied. I longed to be a doctor or a vet, and I knew I was intelligent, so I decided to study and try to do it for myself. I went to night classes to get the qualifications to go to

237

college, then I went to college to get the qualifications to go to university. I studied zoology and geology. I sailed through my exams, but it was hard balancing everything. I had to work every hour I could to make the money for university as I wasn't eligible for a grant (my parents had refused to sign the forms which would have given me some funding). I worked constantly but I was still having flashbacks, I was still facing all my demons. I needed to keep going.

I met someone when I worked in the garage. Harry was one of the good guys. He was kind and patient. We shared the same political views, and we both wanted to make the world a better place. My hang-ups didn't bother him; he just stayed solid and decent throughout everything.

Harry and I stayed together, but it was clear that I couldn't juggle everything. With perfect grades, I was forced to leave university after two years. I didn't have the money, despite having the brains. I was angry about that. I still am. I think I would have made a good doctor, I would have helped people and I would have known how to read between the lines, but that was stolen from me.

Although I lost my chance of going into medicine when I left university, there was a bigger change happening in my life. I had always thought I would never want children. This was for two main reasons. The first was that I didn't know how I would protect them. How could anyone keep a child safe when there were such dangers lurking everywhere, and when those dangers were often within the family itself? This was linked to the second terror. I read a lot of articles and books which said that survivors of abuse often – usually – became abusers themselves. Was that in me? Did I have the capacity to hurt children because I had been hurt? I was sure it wasn't the case, as I had never felt anything like it, but what if becoming a parent brought it out? What if I became my mother, or worse?

Being with Harry changed that. I wanted a family when I was with him. I wanted to challenge the people who said that I would turn into an abuser; I wanted to show that I could love and be loved. It was terrifying, even though it was the most natural thing in the world, but it was what I desperately wanted.

When I found out I was pregnant at 25, it was a miracle. I'd had no idea whether I had been damaged by all of the abuse done to me, or whether I could even have children. The fact that I was pregnant by a man I loved seemed beyond my wildest dreams. I promised myself – and the baby – that I would confound the critics. I would be the mother I had never had, and I would always protect this baby. Harry was fantastic. He got me through my fears, and he was incredibly supportive. We worked as a team, and by the time I was five months pregnant and showing, there was a small voice in my head whispering hope to me.

Maybe, just maybe, I could do this.

At 21 weeks, I knew something was wrong.

It was my first pregnancy, but the baby had been moving for a while and I was used to its patterns each day. When those patterns changed, slowed down and then stopped, I knew something wasn't right.

I went to hospital and was told the baby had died.

There was no kindness in those days when a woman suffered still birth or the loss of a child in the womb. Now, quite rightly, good hospitals have practices in place which offer a chance to mourn. Grief is recognised and worked through, parents get to hold their little ones and take as much time as they need with them. In the 1970s, it was very different. I was told the baby was dead and that I'd have to deliver 'it'.

I did. It was one of the most heartbreaking things I've ever done. At the end of it, the baby was swept away and I wasn't even told if it was a boy or a girl. That was my first child, and I don't even know what it was. I was told to get over it.

When the doctor came in to see me, he asked why I was crying. I could barely speak. His response to me was heartless. 'You're not married, are you?' he said. 'Well, what do you expect?'

I was back to where I had started. Other people were pushing their ideas of God and God's will onto me. It was made quite clear that I had been immoral to be pregnant while I was unmarried, and that I was paying the price. For a while, I wondered whether to believe this. Was I so wrecked inside that I had been responsible for what had happened to my baby? Was it somehow the result of what had been done to me as a child?

I was sent home and told to forget it. But that wasn't possible. I haemorrhaged and developed a horrendous infection within days. I was taken back to hospital where, again, there was no sympathy or support. I asked whether all of this meant that I wouldn't be able to have children and, again, I was told to get married.

Harry and I weren't married for our own reasons. Neither of us was religious, and we both had strong political opinions. I had become aware of feminist ideas while in London, and they helped me make sense of what had happened to me as a child. It seemed hypocritical to marry; and I, more than anyone, had seen what hypocrisy could do to people. Yet, now I was being told that marriage would protect me, marriage would give me healthy babies, marriage would have stopped my baby from dying. It was just a pack of lies. I had been lied to so much for so long, and I couldn't face it happening again.

I looked for reasons — why had the baby really died? — and all I could see was that it was my fault. This was my punishment. Survivors do that with everything. If something good happens, they think they don't deserve it and they did nothing to bring it on. If something bad happens, they think they did bring it on and it is exactly what they deserve. I deserved what had happened to me, and I deserved to lose my baby. This was compounded by what the doctors were saying. I wasn't worthy of good things. I was still dirty; I was still nothing.

I fought hard against those thoughts. I knew now that I wanted a family, my own family, so much. The following year, with Harry's support, I decided that it was time to try for another baby. When I found out I was pregnant, I launched into reading and researching as much as possible

241

about pregnancy and childbirth. Ever since I escaped from the abuse, that has always been my strategy – know as much as possible about as many things as possible. Read, read, read. Learn, learn, learn. If I know things, I can make my own choices, and it is vital for any survivor to have that control.

What I decided then was that I wanted to have a home birth. If this baby was to have the best chance possible, I needed to feel I was making the right decisions for the pair of us. I couldn't face the hospital. I couldn't face their judgement or the invasiveness of the procedures. I read as much as I could about home birth – and there was no Internet back then, so it was much harder to get information – and I just knew it was the right decision for both of us. I would be in a secure and known environment. Harry would be there for me throughout. It felt right.

I was told I was wrong.

I was told that I wanted my baby to die.

Irrespective of how much I explained to the health professionals that this was what I needed and that being in control would be the best option for me, they ignored everything I said. 'Your last baby died,' I was informed, as if I had forgotten that. 'Do you want this one to die as well? Stop being so selfish.'

I was being anything but selfish. I was trying to give us both a chance, especially the baby.

It was a horrific nine months. I was ill throughout and still having flashbacks. I did expect the baby to die, as I thought I hadn't been punished enough. I also thought I would never hold my own child in my arms; I didn't think I would ever be that lucky.

I did it. I had a home birth and I did hold my baby in my arms. Marley was the most beautiful, perfect child. When she was born, I couldn't take my eyes off her.

I was so happy, so content – but I was terrified of her. What if this little girl was the one who would show me just what a monster I was? What if I hurt her? Even if I didn't abuse her, what if I dropped her? She seemed so tiny and vulnerable, and I wanted to protect her from the world. But, what if I was the one she needed to be protected from?

I never doubted my love for Marley but I did doubt whether I was a good mother. I didn't know how to cuddle her, as I had never experienced that myself. I breastfed her, knowing this would bring me contact with her without me even having to think about it. When she lay there, happily feeding, I marvelled at how perfect she was and at the fact that I was giving her what she needed, but I still found it hard to do so many natural things. I never let her cry. I never left her alone with anyone. I never let her out of my sight.

When Marley was two, I had my second child. Matthew was born at home as well. By then, I was better at fighting for my rights. I still didn't know what to do, but I knew what not to do. I remember one day, when he was a tiny baby, reading a parenting magazine. I still absorbed every bit of information I could about everything, always thinking that the answers were out there, if only I could find them. Marley was in her room, playing quietly, and Matthew was asleep after a feed. The article I read sticks in my mind even now – it screamed at me that mothers who didn't cuddle their children were damaging them. I threw the magazine on the floor and rushed through to Marley. I swept her up in my arms and hugged her tightly. The poor little thing looked completely shocked and just wriggled away after a while to continue playing.

Had I hurt them forever by not cuddling them enough, I feared? I had to learn how to do everything as I'd had no role models. I learned from my children more than anyone else, really – I followed their lead, and their natural instincts and I got there. My son Keiran and daughter Jerricah were also born at home; in fact, when Jerricah was born, the other three all sat on the bed as she came into the world. There is a wonderful closeness to that sort of experience and I feel very lucky that I was able to achieve it.

I have still never been able to trust anyone with my children, though. I never let them wander around or be away from me. I didn't terrify them with tales of what had happened to me, but I did give them clear boundaries about what they should do in any given situation. How could I trust anyone? Andrew had been trusted. He was perfect – everyone said so – and yet he had abused that trust in the most heinous way imaginable.

It wasn't until Jerricah, my youngest, was five that I allowed a sleepover. Until then, the four of my children had always gone everywhere as a gang. I suppose I thought there was safety in numbers, and they were all well-trained, so to speak. Jerricah went overnight to a very close friend and I spent all night on the phone. Thankfully, my friend knew this would be the case, and we had both spoken about it, but I still spent the night in a cold sweat. It had taken me that long to allow one of my children to do something which is perfectly natural and commonplace for every other parent, and I still couldn't really manage it.

I didn't want to stifle my children, but I knew the dangers better than anyone. I couldn't share my past with them, but it was exhausting keeping a constant lookout, raising them well, while also dealing with what was going on in my head. I also had to make a decision about my own parents. We all still lived in Dundee and I had to reach my own peace about whether my children would have a relationship with their granny and granddad. Despite everything, I couldn't deny them that. I wanted them to have a 'normal' life and this would be part of that life. I never left them alone with them, and I never let my defences down, but, in the end, they had a great relationship with their grandparents. The way people are as parents can often be very different to how they are as grandparents, and it wasn't my place to stop my children from being loved by others, as long as it was done in a way I was comfortable with. I also thought that, if I kept my children away from their grandparents, they would go looking for them one day. This way, I could tell them what the rules were – and if they wanted to see my kids, they would commit to keeping them safe at all times. They had failed me and I had to live with that, but they would never, ever be allowed to endanger my children.

Mum was a brilliant granny and they all have good, fun memories of her. I told her she could never lift a hand to them, and she kept to that – which shows me that she could control her anger. She had played up to the hot-headed stereotype for years, claiming that she was at the mercy of her own temper, but that was clearly a lie. It only kicked in when it suited her and, to my knowledge, she never hit Sharron either.

Harry and I raised four wonderful children together and he supported me through many difficult times. During our time together, I had started to work with support groups such as Rape Crisis and Women's Aid. When Marley was four, the age I had been when the abuse really began, it brought home to me just how vulnerable a child of that age was. My own childhood was being played out in front of me, in contrast with her life and it made me think more clearly than I had ever done.

For fifteen years, I worked as a volunteer with those groups. I was becoming more and more political as time went on, too, and I protested at Greenham Common and at Faslane. I hated unfairness and inequality. Harry and I set up an alternative bookshop, we went on marches and protests, we helped anyone we could. I would always regret not being a doctor or a vet, but I was discovering other ways to help. I was finding my niche.

I had been working in the centres for a while but slowly all the places for people to go to get help with the after-effects of abuse were closing. So, along with a friend, I did all the training courses I could and offered to run a centre.

The keys were practically thrown at us. It was a baptism of fire, but the ethos of the centre back then was to be led by the grass roots. All I needed to do was listen. I did. I coped. It all grew. Politicians came and went, policies were written, implemented or discarded, and I learned a lot. I learned how to compile reports and apply for funding; I ran courses and started up educational programmes. I knew better than anyone that there were many different aspects of the problem that needed to be addressed, so I looked at issues of violence, too, and I began to provide the same services we offered women to men as well. Abuse knows no boundaries, and I didn't think we should either.

My past hadn't disappeared, but neither did it control my life. I was using what I had been through to help others, and it was helping me, too. I had heard so many stories, so many tales of ruined lives, but I had also witnessed incredible bravery and strength. The most difficult thing for me was when I spoke with people whose stories had similarities to my own.

One day in 2003, the story was just too close for comfort.

As I listened to a young girl pouring her heart out, a thought ran across my mind. Not for the first time, I wondered, is she talking about Andrew?

Abusers don't stop. They die or they're caught. He was still out there – I had seen him in Dundee, although I always walked away when I caught sight of him. I would never have dreamed of talking to him or having any inter-action. But I couldn't imagine that he had suddenly stopped what he had taken such pleasure from.

That day it was as if something switched inside my head. Sod this, I thought. It's time to talk.

I had sorted my head out by that time in my life. I had children and a home. I had credibility. That day, I phoned Sharron.

'I've never spoken to anyone else about it and you need to make up your own mind about what you want to do, but . . . I'm going to the police.'

I left her to mull it over and I made a second call.

I had friends in the police and I knew some things about what I was going to do. I didn't want to talk to someone I knew, and I didn't want to talk to someone who took statements whenever we had a case at the support group. It would have been impossible for me to tell all of my story to someone I knew.

It was arranged that I would go to Perth to give my statement. I did that within the week. There was something driving me to do this and I knew there was no turning back. My youngest son took me to the police station – all he knew, all my whole family knew, was that I had been abused. I had never told them who had done it, or the details. When it came up, I simply said that I had had a really bad childhood.

I went in, gave my statement, and watched as it was placed in an envelope, then sealed. It took four hours.

I wasn't prepared for the aftermath – certainly not the aftermath for me personally.

It is hard to stay silent about something this big for so many years and then verbalise it. In some ways, you are protected by the silence. Now, it was all stirred up in my head and I had to relive my past. But I still didn't feel I could talk to anyone. I left the police station, didn't call my son, and went to sit by the river as my head was full of thoughts and memories of things I had tried to push away and things I would never forget.

I didn't expect it to affect me so much. I was strong. I had survived. I thought nothing could touch me. So why did I feel traumatised? Why did I feel drained? I was so used to helping other people, but I had nothing with which I could help myself.

When I finally felt I could go home, I tried to carry on with a normal life, but it was hard. I knew that I would have to go through it all again in court. As time went on, I was hearing that other people were coming forward; more victims. I had also decided before I gave the statement that I would only deal with the abuse by Andrew, so this was an issue I needed to process. I knew that if I spoke of the ritual abuse, I would be discredited. I worked in this area; I knew how things played out. Only a few years earlier, there had been a witch-hunt against anyone who opened up the debate about organised abuse; people and agencies had been attacked, and I knew no one would believe my story. It was all about labels. I was fully aware that a lawyer standing up in court saying, 'We have a survivor of child sexual abuse here,' was treated very differently to one who said, 'We have a survivor of ritual sexual abuse here.'

I couldn't risk it.

I couldn't risk Andrew getting away with it, even if it

meant my story would not be heard fully, and the other people responsible for my childhood abuse would not be brought to justice.

Just before the trial, Mum called me. She was very upset as she had been called as a witness.

'I'm not going!' she said. 'I won't do it!'

I waited until she had shouted herself out.

'Do you know what this is?' I asked her.

She didn't reply.

'This is an opportunity. It's an opportunity for you to redeem yourself.'

She stayed silent.

'If you do this, if you do the right thing, I will have no issues with you. It will all be over,' I told her.

I meant it. I wanted her to stand by Sharron. My sister had told her, she had told everyone, and no one had believed her. She had gone to her when she was raped, and she was told to put some cream on. She had informed Mum of what Andrew was doing, and Mum had said he was missing his wife.

None of that could be changed. But Sharron needed Mum to do this one thing.

And to her credit, she did it.

She turned up at court and gave a statement which supported everything we said. I didn't see her, as I only went to court to do my bit and then left; but I kept to my word. In my eyes, Mum had redeemed herself.

Sharron asked me if I would go back to court for Andrew's sentencing, and I did. He stared at me when I looked at him, and I felt sorry for the old, pitiful man who had ruined my childhood.

I also felt angry.

The man who had abused me was not this man. He had been young and strong. I wanted that man to be in the dock. This man was pathetic, but he had also lived his life unscathed, unlike me. I felt pity and anger. I wanted him to admit it, but he wouldn't.

Andrew was found guilty but, even then, he wouldn't admit it. We were given another date for sentencing and told that background reports would be prepared. All of this was done – without asking us about anything at all, as is always the case – but then we were given the devastating news that he was going to appeal.

The background reports had been a joke. He was deemed to be low risk. This was decided by talking to him, not by talking to the victims – isn't that the most ridiculous thing? No one asked us, no one asked the victims. Would you decide that a proven burglar was low risk by talking to the burglar? No – but I guess that things are more important than people, than children.

The appeal was put in process and while we waited for it to happen, he was sent to Peterhead for three and a half years. Three and a half years for what he did to me, to Sharron, and to the others. It's a joke.

I had my life taken from me. I would have been a vet or a doctor. I don't regret how I've used my life, but I do regret that I wasn't allowed to choose my own path.

The appeal loomed in my mind. I was so sure he would

get away with it. The only reason he had been convicted was because I had witnessed him raping Sharron, and now he was challenging that. When I gave evidence that second time, it was the worst experience of my adult life. The lawyers tried to damage my credibility by making fun of me. They said, 'You're asking us to believe you did nothing to help your sister?'

I said, 'Yes.' I had to. It was the truth.

They laughed at the thought that they were expected to believe it.

They said that I was a feminist and that my job proved I was out to 'get' men.

I knew how the system worked. I didn't rise to anything, and I kept all of my answers to 'yes' and 'no'.

Again, my mother gave evidence.

Again, we went through it all.

The retrial took as long as the first court case.

I was demonised and it was all made to sound unbelievable. I knew I couldn't mention a word of the ritual abuse or it would all fall down.

I was prepared for him to win.

I wasn't prepared for him to be found guilty again, but he was. He was!

The court didn't hear all of my story, but they heard some of it and that has to be enough for me. This book tells some more, but not all – I have to tell my life in parts. It wasn't so long ago that we found it hard – some found it impossible – to believe that fathers could rape their children. Through the bravery of some incredible people, the world had to sit up and take notice. Maybe that day will come for those who have survived ritual abuse, too.

There came a time when I was working with two survivors of ritual abuse and I had to lie low, as I was receiving threats. I was unable to go into work and unable to leave the house at many points, as some people objected to the help I was giving to these women, but I had to do something. Of course, I was trying to help both of them as much as I could, but I was also becoming very frustrated with what I was hearing over and over again, and what no one was listening to. These people were trying to escape from their families, and everything was uncertain. The two young women were unrelated to each other and from separate groups, even different towns, but they needed the same thing – a safe refuge. They both stayed with me for a while and so much of what I uncovered was, to many I'm sure, unbelievable. Even when experiencing the reality, it was quite difficult to believe all that was happening.

Both of the young women who were trying to escape did get away from their abusers. They stayed away and they managed to thrive, and so did I. That's what matters, that's what I hold onto.

At a time when many critics are questioning the motivation and benefit of survivor memoirs, I hope this book will challenge and silence them all. As an internationally renowned expert in abuse and violence prevention and support, I have chosen to detail my own personal journey to help others. It hasn't been easy.

Every time someone discloses their abuse to me and discovers that I, too, was in that situation, they say the same thing: they say they would never have believed it. I want every survivor, every victim, to know that this happens to so many people. It was never their fault, it never is. If I don't speak, how can I tell others to find the courage to do the same? If telling my story helps one child, it's worth it.

Towards the end of her life, my mum finally called me Laurie and tried to engage with me. I couldn't do it. I couldn't forget or wipe out what her years of neglect had left me open to. I could be civil to her for the sake of her grandchildren, but there would be no big reunion or emotional scene of forgiveness. How could I forgive her?

When Mum was in her last days, I tried to remember good things about her. She'd always had a lovely voice and adored music. I thought back to how she would sing or play her Jim Reeves records around the house. She was capable of happiness, I had seen it back then; it just never seemed related to me. Every good memory was tainted. When I thought of her beautiful singing voice, I recalled that everyone on both sides of my family was very musically talented. Apart from me. All of the children were sent to music classes and everyone could play an instrument. Apart from me. When I was young, they all sang together. Apart from me. Any time I did sing, I was told I was tone deaf and should shut up. Any time I expressed an interest in learning to play the piano, my mum would ask what was the point?

Even the joy I could have got from music had been denied me.

Mum and Dad used to sing in working men's clubs and go to ballroom dancing sessions. I tried to cling on to those memories of her as a normal woman, but the sense of being different was still so strong. The sensible side of me could see that I was different because I'd been treated differently, but it was still hard. The feelings of inadequacy and inferiority were still there. The only thing she had ever said about me that was positive was that I was clever, but even that was twisted. Her voice telling me I was 'too clever for your own good' rang in my ears.

Mum got very ill towards the end and I longed for her to make amends. She had done what she could during the court case and that had taken a lot. I actually think she was amazing for what she did then, but it was all I was going to get. I was never what she wanted. As I sat watching her fade, I remembered the good-looking woman who had been so ashamed of her plain little girl. I remembered the way she would angrily knot a ribbon in my hair in an attempt to make me look like a girl, as she would say. I had never reached her standards or expectations of what a daughter should be. I did what I could before she died. I was a dutiful daughter and I looked after her, but there is no happy ending, I'm afraid. We didn't forget our differences. She didn't tell me she loved me and was sorry. She died and I went on with my life. It's as simple and as unsatisfying as that.

Life doesn't always have happy endings when we want

them, but we can try to make our own. I hope everyone who reads this book will do that for themselves. I'll help you if I can because it is so important to live your life. Abusers can take so much, but they can't take everything.

I have so much. A lot was taken, but I have more.

So do you.

You just have to believe it.

EPILOGUE

SAVING LAURIE

My story didn't end when I left home and it didn't end with Andrew's conviction or my mother's death – but, then again, I probably have another dozen books in me. I've lived enough for many lives but what I've told you here will have to do for now. I've never been desperate to tell my story; perhaps because I've been so busy trying to help others come to terms with their own lives, any value my own story might have has never really been too important in my mind. However, a few months ago, I mentioned something to my youngest daughter, just a passing remark about when I was fourteen and living on the streets.

'You should write your book, Mum,' she said.

I laughed it off – but it stuck in my mind and made me think.

Maybe I should. So many times, I've dealt with young people who think that their abuse is a shameful thing. They

257

often blame themselves, and they fear they'll never get past it, never be able to move on from what was done to them. I don't keep quiet about what happened to me, I talk about it when it's relevant, and when the court case was ongoing, I waived my right to anonymity, but I've also shied away from telling everything. That is partly because my job is to listen. When someone comes to me, they need to talk, they need to be heard, or they just need to sit there in silence until they know they're in a safe place. I've always thought that I don't need to fill up their heads with what happened to me. But when Jerricah made that comment, I wondered . . . What if my talking made it better for someone else?

It means a lot to survivors when they see someone who appears to have made something of their life, or who has 'dealt' with it. In the midst of their own hurt or fear or confusion, they sometimes think that 'victim' will be the only label ever applied to them.

Do I have a message for anyone reading this book? Of course I do! It's my reason for writing it in the first place. There is hope. Really, I do mean that. Bad things happened to me, I don't deny that, but I'm still standing. I'm still doing my damnedest every day.

They didn't manage to destroy me. I've still been able to help people, perhaps not in the way I wanted to, but I'd like to think I've done my bit.

I firmly believe that you can face your fear and use it, or you can go under. I won't ever give them the satisfaction of me going under.

When I was writing this book, someone asked me if I allowed myself to feel proud of what I've done. The answer has to be no because I haven't done it alone. All of my achievements at the groups I run are a team effort. I always have a feeling that I could do more, that I could have done more. I still feel that I'm not a terribly worthwhile person sometimes. But there is so much to do, so much to fight for – maybe there will come a day when I do think, 'You've done quite well, Laurie, you've done quite well.'

I have written things in this book which I thought I would never share with anyone. What has really hit me as I have done that, is the awareness that not very much has changed at all. In fact, some things are worse. These days, we have a perception that child abuse is being tackled. We have policies and papers and working groups, but there is still nowhere for a child to go. What I want more than anything is for there to be a way for survivors to get away at an early age. If I was fourteen now, going through what I went through, there would still be nowhere for me to turn. Children are still not listened to, but because there is the perception that they are being listened to, things are very bad for them.

I will always do whatever I can for anyone in need. I don't care if it's a man or a woman, an adult or a child; if they need my help, I'll be there.

I have peace and love in my life. I'm surrounded by my own children and my grandchildren. I never thought I'd have all of that. I still don't think I deserve it. I feel so lucky to have survived and have all of this. Every day, I tell myself how good life is, and how good my life is.

That's special. I made that for myself and no one can ever take it away from me.

I did it.

I saved Laurie.

ACKNOWLEDGEMENTS

Although this story is my own, many people have helped to bring it to fruition. I've known for years that I have a tale to tell, but also that there would come a day when it was the right time to tell it. My youngest daughter Jerricah was the one who pointed out that the day had come. I'd like to thank her for her encouragement and wisdom.

All of my children have been loyal and loving throughout this process. I have no idea whether they will ever read the book, but they now have that option. We've been through so much together – a book in itself! – and they have fought many battles with me, against prejudice and bigotry, against unfairness and ignorance.

To Marley, Matthew, Keiran, Jerricah and Nicole – thank you.

261

My partner has been a constant source of support to me for many years in everything I do.

In telling my story, I have said many things which I've never spoken out loud before. I've told things which I thought I'd never tell another human being. Not all of those things have been included in this book, but they've all been listened to by one person, my ghost writer, Linda Watson-Brown. I'd like to thank her for what she's done, and for the way in which she's done it. The book would not be in your hands now without her creativity, sensitivity and support.

Within the process of writing this book, I have been helped by Clare Hulton, Kerri Sharp, and all at Simon and Schuster.

Over the years, every person who has come through the doors of the charity has given me the strength to keep going. Even at difficult times – and there have been many – I have known that this is the right thing to do. As I've fought for funding, made our case to politicians, spoken at international conferences, and travelled the globe, there has been only one thing driving me – if I can help one child, I will.

They have all helped me in their own ways, too. I intend to put aside a copy of this book for my grandchildren and foster children to read when they are older, to help them

Acknowledgements

understand me better and let them know that hardships
and adversity in childhood can be overcome.

Thank you for reading – and thank you if you can make a
difference, too.

Laurie Matthew

HELP AND SUPPORT FROM LAURIE

If you have been affected by any of the issues raised in *Groomed*, you can access help and support through the various groups I have established.

Eighteen And Under is a voluntary organisation which was founded in 1994. It provides long-term confidential support for young people aged eighteen and under who have been abused in any way. This abuse includes sexual abuse, physical abuse, domestic abuse, ritual abuse and emotional abuse. The most common abuse we work with is sexual abuse. www.18u.org.uk

In addition to support work with young people, we also work at ending all violence and abuse. We have developed a range of evidence-based educational resources and materials for use with all ages of young people and vulnerable adults. The programme is called the V.I.P. – Violence Is

Preventable – Project. This project has won local, national and international awards for innovation and achievement. The V.I.P. Project resources are currently rolling out into nurseries, primary schools and high schools across the UK and now even into other countries, including Kenya, Cameroon, Palestine, Zambia, Poland and Pakistan. www.violenceispreventable.org.uk

Izzy's Promise is a charity which was founded in 2002. The need for this service was quickly identified, following the publication of several books on the subject of ritual and organised abuse. It offers support to survivors of ritual and organised abuse through a website, helpline and face-to-face services. It provides training and awareness for other agencies and increasingly works with agencies across the UK to tackle exploitation, organised abuse and trafficking. www.izzyspromise.org.uk

www.rans.org.uk
Ritual abuse network survivors.

18 Plus was founded in 2009 and is a registered charity. It provides support to male survivors of sexual and domestic abuse and is currently developing services for elderly people affected by abuse and violence. It was formed to address the gap in services for male survivors and older people. www.adultsurvivor.org.uk

The support provided by all the organisations is similar

and depends on the needs and wishes of the survivor. No appointments are necessary and survivors can drop in whenever they are in need or in crisis. We present an open-door policy with no need for survivors to identify themselves to us or share any personal information. Any records kept are minimal and completely open to the survivors. We work at the pace of the survivor and support them in trying to find their own solutions to their problems. Often we accompany survivors to the police or courts if this is what they want. We have an extremely high degree of confidentiality and do not report anything survivors say to any other person or agency unless someone is at serious risk of harm.

LAURIE'S AWARDS

Some of the many awards given have been:

Charity Awards 2010 Winner of Research, Advice and Support Category

The Guardian Charity Awards 2010 Shortlisted (Izzy's Promise)

Charity Times Award Shortlisted 2010

Social Justice Awards 2007 Highly Commended

Crimestoppers Community Unity Award for Community Safety 2006 (award for Laurie personally)

Scottish Social Services Care Accolades 2006 Special Commendation for Good Practice

Community Care Award (Older People Category) Finalist 2006

Dubai International Awards 2006 V.I.P. Project classified as 'Promising Practice'

Dundee Partnership Community Safety Award 2005

Charity Awards Highly Commended Research Advice and Support 2005 (Izzy's Promise)

Beacon Fellowship 2004 Shortlisted in the category of risk-taking (award for Laurie personally)

International Women's Safety Award 2004

GlaxoSmithKline International Impact Award 2003 (for V.I.P. Project)

Queen's Golden Jubilee Award 2003 (for Eighteen And Under)

Finalist Community Care Child Protection Award 2003 (for V.I.P. Project)

Charity Awards Highly Commended 2003 (for V.I.P. Project)

Camelot Oyster Awards Regional Winner 2002 for V.I.P. Project (award for Laurie personally)

Finalist National Oyster Awards 2002 for V.I.P. Project (award for Laurie personally)

Shortlisted Community Care Award for Child Protection 2002 (for V.I.P. Project)

Community Care Award for Child Protection 2000 (for V.I.P. Project)

Junior Chambers Scotland Young Scotland Award 1999

Whitbread Volunteer Action Award Youth Winner 1998

Whitbread Volunteer Action Award Regional Winner 1998

Dundee Citizen of the Year 1997 (award for Laurie personally)

PUBLISHER'S NOTICE

Laurie's story contains many deeply shocking and traumatic events. Although her uncle, Andrew, served three years in prison for his crimes, no one else has ever been brought to account or faced charges for the abuses of Laurie and of other unknown children in the Dundee area during the early 1960s.

If, having read her story, you think you were one of the other children who suffered at the hands of the people described in this book, then we recommend you contact Dundee Police on 0300 111 2222 or email: mail@tayside.pnn.police.uk or you could contact Crimestoppers on 0800 555 111.